INDEFINITE LEAVE

'14년 거주
영주권 제도'는

TO REMAIN (**ILR**) IS
A FORM OF AMNESTY
WHICH ALLOWS

영국에 14년 이상 거주한
장기 체류자가 합법적으로

OVERSTAYERS TO
LEGALISE THEIR STAY
IN THE UK AFTER

영국에 거주할 수 있도록
허용하는 사면 제도다.

14 YEARS.

HOWEVER, IT HAS
BEEN ABOLISHED.

그러나 이 제도는
폐지됐다.

AND NOW

이제 이 자격을 얻으려면
20년이 소요된다.

REQUIRES **20** YEARS.

INDEFINITE LEAVE TO REMAIN (ILR) IS A FORM OF AMNESTY WHICH ALLOWS OVERSTAYERS TO LEGALISE THEIR STAY IN THE UK AFTER 14 YEARS.

HOWEVER, IT HAS BEEN ABOLISHED.

AND NOW REQUIRES 20 YEARS.

서문

'14년 거주 영주권'(이하 '14년 규정') 제도가 '20년 거주 영주권'(이하 '20년 규정') 제도로 전환되기 직전, '꿈꾸는 불법자'(illegal dreamers)라는 주제로, 그들의 삶과 현실을 객관적으로, 그리고 심층적으로 들여다보기 위해 이민 전문 법률가와 일곱 명의 전(前) 불법 이민자를 만났습니다. 그 후, 이들과의 인터뷰 내용을 바탕으로 2013년 영국왕립예술대학(Royal College of Art)에서 학위 논문을 발표하면서 소량의 단행본을 출간했습니다. 저는 인권에 관한 생각을, '자유'의 소중함을, 그리고 체류 기간을 20년 이상 연장해 가며 자신의 '꿈'을 좇아 살아온 이들의 이야기를 더 많은 이들과 나누고 싶었습니다. 그리고 2024년, 프로파간다 출판사의 도움으로 10년 전 프로젝트를 한국어 번역본으로 재출간하게 됐습니다.

이들의 이야기는 시간이 지나도 인간의 존엄과 정의를 상징하고, 동시에 자유, 인권, 연대와 같은 다양한 주제에 대한 생각을 자극합니다. 이 프로젝트를 통해 우리가 불안과 고통으로 점철된 이들의 삶을 더 가까이 들여다보기를, 그래서 인간 존재에 관한 근본적인 질문을 다시 던지고, 개인의 경험을 초월하는 연결고리를 발견하기를 희망합니다.

Preface

Just before the transition from the '14-year Indefinite Leave to Remain (the 14 year rule)' to the '20-year Indefinite Leave to Remain (the 20 year rule)' in the UK, I met with seven former illegal immigrants and specialized immigration solicitors to objectively and deeply explore the lives and realities of 'illegal dreamers.' Based on these interviews, I published a book in a small edition as my degree show at the Royal College of Art in 2013. Before starting the longer stories of those who have lived for over 20 years pursuing their 'dreams' under the extended legal residency, I wanted to share the importance of 'freedom' and thoughts on human rights with more people. Therefore, with the help of Propaganda Publishing in 2024, I revisited this work from ten years ago, republishing it with a Korean translation.

Their stories, embodying human dignity and justice, continue to inspire reflection on freedom, human rights, and empathy. Through lives riddled with anxiety and suffering, these narratives challenge us to revisit core questions about human existence and seek connections that transcend personal experiences.

서문

14년 거주 영주권(이하 '14년 규정')에서 '20년 거주 영주권(이하 '20년 규정')' 제도로 전환되기 직전 [redacted] 이민 전문 변호사와 함께 영국 불법 이민자 7명을 만났습니다. 그 후, 이들과의 인터뷰 내용을 바탕으로 2013년 영국 왕립예술대학(Royal College of Art)에서 학위 논문을 발표하면서 소량의 단행본을 출간했습니다. [redacted]

이들의 이야기는 [redacted] 이 프로젝트를 통해 우리가 불안과 고통으로 점철된 이들의 삶을 더 가까이 들여다보기를, 그래서 인간 존재에 대한 근본적인 질문을 다시 던지고 개인의 경험을 초월하는 연결고리를 발견하기를 희망합니다.

Preface

Just before the transition from the '14-year Indefinite Leave to Remain (the 14-year rule)' to the '20-year Indefinite Leave to Remain (the 20-year rule)' in the UK, I met with seven former illegal immigrants and specialized immigration solicitors [redacted] Based on these interviews, I published a book in a small edition as my degree show at the Royal College of Art in 2013. [redacted] Therefore, with the help of Propaganda Publishing in 2024, I revisited this work from ten years ago, republishing it with a Korean translation.

Their stories, embodying [redacted] Through lives riddled with anxiety and suffering, these narratives challenge us to revisit core questions about human existence and seek connections that transcend personal experiences.

대규모 이민을 최우선 의제로 삼는 나라가 많다. 이민 정책을 논할 때 불법 이민 문제를 떼어 놓을 수 없기에 이민 정책에는 항상 논란이 따른다. 이 프로젝트는 영국 정부가 시행했던 불법 이민자 사면법인 '14년 규정'에 관한 호기심에서 시작됐다. '14년 규정'은, 영국에 일정 기간 이상 거주한 장기 체류자들에게 영주권(Indefinite Leave to Remain, ILR)을 부여함으로써 이들의 합법 체류를 허용하는 제도로, 5년 거주, 10년 거주, 14년 거주 등 세 가지 범주에 해당하는 불법 및 합법 장기 체류자에게 적용됐다. 이 프로젝트에서 구체적으로 다룰 '14년 규정'이 제정된 배경에는 다음과 같은 조항을 강조하는 인권법이 있다.

"모든 사람은 박해를 피해 다른 나라에서 피난처를 구할 권리와 그것을 누릴 권리를 가진다." [1]

"모든 사람은 자신의 사생활과 가정생활, 주거 및 통신을 존중받을 권리가 있다." [2]

1. 세계인권선언 제14조.

2. 1998년 인권법: 이 법은 영국법 내에서 인권 조약 위반에 대한 구제책을 마련하여 영국 법원에서 인권 협약을 위반한 사례에 대한 구제를 제공하고, 이로써 스트라스부르 유럽인권재판소 출두의 필요성을 소거한다.

위 조항에 근거하여 제정된 '14년 규정'에 따라 영국에 14년 이상 거주한 자는 영국 내무부(UK Home Office)에 ILR을 신청할 수 있게 됐다. 노동당이 이 정책을 도입한 2003년 이래로 약 9000명의 불법 이민자가 사면 혜택을 받았다. 그러나 이후 '14년 규정'이 폐지됐다.[3] 영국 국경청(UK Border Agency)은 "단순히 몇 년 동안 단속을 피했다고 해서 영국에 체류할 권리를 얻어서는 안 되며, 영국에 정착하는 것은 특권"이라며 합법적인 거주를 위한 필수 체류

3. 2012년 7월 9일 이후 제출된 모든 신청이 취소됐다.

Many governments put mass immigration at the very top of their agendaImmigration is a controversial issue at present because it involves talking about illegal immigrants. This project started out from curiosity about a form of amnesty, the 14-year rule, in the UK. The 14-year rule allowed overstayers to legalise their stay in the UK as Indefinite Leave to Remain (ILR) after a certain number of years, which applied to three categories of illegal or legal overstayers: those who had overstayed for 5 years, 10 years and 14 years. Specifically, the 14-year rule, we will talk about, was established considering the following aspects of human rights law:

"Everyone has the right to seek and to enjoy in other countries asylum from persecution"[1] and "Everyone has the right to respect for his private and family life, his home and his correspondence."[2]

1. Article 14 of the Universal Declaration of Human Rights.

2. Human Rights Act 1998: The Act provides a remedy for breaches of a Convention right in UK courts, eliminating the need to go to the European Court of Human Rights in Strasbourg.

Under this human rights law, after 14 years, one could apply for 'Indefinite Leave to Remain' (ILR) at the UK Home Office. Since the Labour Party introduced this policy in 2003, about 9,000 illegal immigrants had been granted such rights. However, the 14-year rule was then abolished.[3] According to the

3. It was abolished for all applications submitted after July 9, 2012.

[illegible]

[redacted]

[redacted]

[illegible] [redacted] [illegible] [redacted] [illegible]

Many governments put their immigration at the very top of their agenda. Immigration is a controversial issue at present because it involves talking about illegal immigrants. This project started out from curiosity about a form of amnesty, the 14-year rule, in the UK. The 14-year rule allowed overstayers to legalise their stay in the UK as Indefinite Leave to Remain (ILR) after a certain number of years, which applied to three categories of illegal or legal overstayers: those who had overstayed for 5 years, 10 years and 14 years. Specifically, the 14-year rule, we will talk about, was [redacted]

[redacted]

Under this human rights law, after 14 years, one could apply for Indefinite Leave to Remain (ILR) at the UK Home Office. Since the Labour Party introduced this policy in 2003, about 9,000 illegal immigrants had been granted such rights. However, [redacted] According to the

기간을 최소 20년으로 대폭 연장했다. 장기 불법 체류자에게 영구 거주권을 부여하는 정부의 정책은 당시 외국인 신분으로 영국에 거주하고 있었던 내게 매우 인상 깊었고, 동시에 몇 가지 궁금증을 유발했다. — 불법 장기 체류자들은 영국에서 ILR을 취득한 이후의 상황에 만족하고 있을까? — 이들은 어떤 이유로 불법 체류하게 됐을까? — 이들을 '불법 체류자' 대신 '꿈을 좇는 자'라고 부를 수 있을까? — 이들에게 자유와 권리를 누릴 자격이 있는 걸까? — 14년이었던 체류 기간을 20년으로 연장한 정책은 합당한가? — 수백만 명의 불법 이민자들을 사면하고 이들에게 영국에 체류할 권리를 주어야 할 이유는 무엇인가? — 수백만 명의 불법 이민자가 음지에서 계속 생활하고 일할 수 있어야 할 이유는 무엇인가? — 영국 정부와 국민은 이민자의 불법 체류를 어떤 시각으로 바라보는가? — 이러한 문제를 심도 있게 조사하기 위하여 여러 법률가를 만나 해당 규정이 제정된 기원과 그 역사를 알아보았으며, '14년 규정'을 통해 ILR을 받은 전 불법 이민자 일곱 명을 만나 인터뷰를 진행했다. 인터뷰는 익명으로 진행했고, 인터뷰 대상자의 신원과 관련한 부분은 당사자의 동의하에 삭제했다. 인터뷰 대상자의 진실한 감정 상태를 최대한 있는 그대로 담아내기 위하여 이들에게 인터뷰 도중에 떠오르는 글이나 그림을 자유롭게 쓰거나 그려 달라고 부탁했다. 그리고 그들의 진정성을 해치지 않기 위해 그들이 작성한 글에서 문법적 오류를 수정하지 않았다. 이 책에 수록된 모든 손글씨와 그림은 인터뷰 대상자가 직접 쓰고 그린 것이다.

이 프로젝트를 진행하면서 '14년 규정'을 향한 상반된 견해가 존재한다는[4] 사실을

4. 이 프로젝트의 설문과 인터뷰 내용을 기반으로 작성된 의견이다. (245쪽)

UK Border Agency, the right to remain in the country "should not be achieved simply by evading our detection for a number of years, and settling in the UK is a privilege," leading to a significant extension of the residence requirement to at least 20 years for legal residency. Granting UK residency rights to long-term illegal residents was very impressive to me, being a foreigner in the UK at the time, and it raised several questions.

So, are illegal overstayers satisfied with their circumstances after being granted ILR in the UK? Which reasons make them stay illegally? Could they be called 'dreamers', not 'illegals'? Do they deserve rights and freedoms? Is the change to 20 years from 14 years reasonable? Also, why should millions of illegal immigrants be given amnesty to stay in the UK? Why should millions of illegal immigrants be able to continue to live and work in the shadows? What is the UK government's and the people's stance on illegality? In order to conduct an in-depth investigation into this matter, met with several solicitors and lawyers to research the origins and history of this law, and I also met seven former illegal immigrants who had received 'ILR' under the crucial 14-year rule for this project. The interviews were conducted anonymously, and parts related to the interviewees'

기간을 최소 20년으로 대폭 연장했다는 것이 불법 체류자에게 영주 자격을 부여하는 정부의 처벌은 당시 외국인 신분으로 영국에 거주하고 있던 내게 매우 인상 깊었고, 동시에 몇 가지 궁금증을 유발했다. — 불법 체류자들은 영주권을 받은 이후의 상황에 만족하고 있을까? — 무슨 이유로 불법 체류를 하게 되었을까? — 그들을 불법 체류자 대신 '꿈을 좇는 자'라고 부를 수 있을까? — 그들에게 자유와 권리를 누릴 자격이 있는 걸까? — 14년에서 20년으로 기간을 늘린 것은 합당한가? — 수백만 명의 불법 이민자들을 사면하고 영국에 머물게 해야 하는 이유는 무엇인가? — 수백만 명의 불법 이민자가 음지에서 계속 생활하고 일할 수 있어야 하는 이유는 무엇인가? — 영국 정부와 국민은 [redacted] 다리고 그들의 감정을 헤아려 [redacted] 왔다 [redacted]

이 프로젝트를 ...

UK Border Agency, the right to remain in the country could not be achieved simply by evading our determination for a number of years, and [redacted] lending to a significant extension of the residence requirement to at least 20 years for legal residency. Granting UK residency rights to long-term illegal residents was very impressive to me, being a foreigner in the UK at the time, and it raised several questions.

So, are illegal overstayers satisfied with their circumstances after being granted ILR in the UK? Which reasons make them stay illegally? Could they be called 'dreamers', not 'illegals'? Do they deserve rights and freedoms? Is the change to 20 years from 14 years reasonable? Also, why should millions of illegal immigrants be given amnesty to stay in the UK? Why should millions of illegal immigrants be able to continue to live and work in the shadows? What is the UK government's and the people's stance on illegality? In order to conduct an in-depth investigation into this matter, I met with several solicitors and lawyers to research the origins and history of this law [redacted] and parts related to the interviewees

알게 됐다. 전 불법 이민자 가운데 일부는 현재 규정에 만족하나, 누구에게도 이를 추천하지 않는다고 답했다. 영국 국민 대다수는 불법 이민에 반대하지만, '14년 규정' 혹은 '20년 규정'에 대해 잘 알지 못한다고 답했다. 한편, 영국 정부는 인권을 존중하면서도 관련 불법 행위에 대해 적절하게 조처하지 않는다. 이민 문제는 인권에 뿌리를 두고 있으면서[5] 여러 사회 문제를 초래하여 논란이 된다.[6] 단일 주제이지만 두 가지 측면을 지닌 문제이기도 하다. 이러한 양면성을 탐구하기 위해 해당 프로젝트는 역 인화기법처럼 다양한 방법을 활용해 문제를 분석했으며, 이를 통해 밝혀낸 사실, 즉 '14년 규정'으로 ILR을 취득한 이들의 숨겨진 실제 이야기를 시각적 언어로 전달하고자 노력했다.

6. 불법 이민과 관련하여 언급되는 문제로는 크게 불법 이민자가 직면하는 위험과 수용 국가가 직면하는 어려움으로 분류할 수 있다.

5. 이 규정은 유럽인권협약 제8조에 근거한다. 조문은 "모든 사람은 자신의 사생활과 가정생활, 주거 및 통신을 존중받을 권리가 있다".

나는 개인적으로 인권 보호 측면에서 '14년 규정'을 존중해야 한다고 생각하지만, 이 프로젝트는 불법 이민을 지지하거나 해당 규정의 폐지를 옹호하지 않는다. 다만, 사면의 형태로서 '14년 규정'이 영국에 얼마나 효과적인 역할을 했는지, 해당 규정에 따라 ILR을 취득한 불법 이민자들은 그 정책에 얼마나 만족했는지, 그들이 어떤 이유로 14년이라는 시간을 희생해야 했는지에 관해 일곱 명의 이야기를 들어 보고자 할 뿐이다. 나아가 이 문제에 대해 여러분이 어떤 의견을 갖게 될지 알고 싶다.

identities were deleted with their consent. During the interviews, in order to capture their genuine emotions and states, they were encouraged to write or draw whatever they felt while speaking. Grammatical errors in their writings were not corrected, preserving the authenticity of their expressions. Thus, all the handwriting and drawings included in this book were created directly by the interviewees.

As I researched the topic, I discovered double-edged views [4] on the rule.Regarding ex-illegal immigrants, some are now satisfied with the rule but would never recommend it to anyone. In terms of British people, almost all are against illegal immigration but are unaware of the rule. Meanwhile, the UK government respects human rights but seriously overlooks illegal activities. The topic is controversial due to its roots in human rights[5] and the associated social problems.[6] There are two sides to this single subject. I attempted to explore this through presswork with opaque paper and reverse printing in my book, aiming to convey the hidden and real stories of people granted ILR under the 14-year rule using visual language. I sought to express the reality of the shadows and the unmentioned aspects of the issue through the media. Personally, I believe the 14-year rule deserves respect from a human rights protection standpoint, but this

4. These opinions are based on surveys and interviews of this project. (page 245)

6. Some perceived problems associated with illegal immigration can be categorised into the dangers faced by unathorised immigrants and the challenges faced by the host or receiving country.

5. This rule is based on Article 8 of the European Convention on Human Rights: "Article 8 protects your right to respect for your private life, your family life, your home and your correspondence"

[illegible]

[redacted]

[illegible]

[redacted]

[illegible]

[redacted] during the interviews. In order to cho[redacted] ture [redacted]

As I researched the topic, I discovered double-edged views on the rule. Regarding ex-illegal immigrants, some are not satisfied with the rule oth[redacted] would never recommend it to anyone. In terms of British people, also sa[redacted] against illegal immigration but are unaware of the rule. Meanwhile, the UK government respects human rights but seriously overlooks illegal activities. The topic is controversial due to its roots in human rights and the associated social problems.[8] [redacted] to conve[redacted] extremely. I believe the 14-year rule deserves respect from a human rights protection standpoint, but this project does not support illegal immigration nor advocate for the abolition of this rule. Instead, it seeks to explore how effective this rule has been in the UK as a form of amnesty, how satisfied illegal immigrants who received ILR under this rule have been, and why they had to sacrifice 14 years. I am curious to hear the stories of seven individuals on these matters and to know what opinion you might have.

[redacted]

EVERYONE HAS THE RIGHT TO SEEK AND TO ENJOY IN OTHER COUNTRIES ASYLUM FROM PERSECUTION.

● 모든 사람은 박해를 피해 다른 나라에서 피난처를 구할 권리와 그것을 누릴 권리를 가진다. — 세계인권선언 제14조

Article 14 — The Universal Declaration of Human Rights.

EVERYONE
HAS

AND

ASYLUM

#1
ANONYMOUS

Please
introduce yourself.

My name is [redacted]
And I M [redacted] years Old

Q. 자기소개 부탁드립니다.

A. 제 이름은 -입니다. 전 -살이에요.

Please
introduce yourself.

Q. 자기소개 부탁드립니다.

A. 제 이름은 -입니다. 전 -살이에요.

How long did it take for you to be granted 'indefinite leave to remain'?

It was for 18 years

Q. 14년 체류 규정을 받기까지 얼마나 걸렸나요?

A. 18년 걸렸습니다.

How long did it take for you to be granted
'indefinite leave to remain'?

It was for 18 years

How long did it take for you to be granted
'indefinite leave to remain'?

Q. 14년 체류 규정을 받기까지 얼마나 걸렸나요?

A. 18년 걸렸습니다.

Have you been to your country since you left?

No, I haven't been my
own country since
I left There is no one
I want to meat
Sometimes I miss my
hometown where I lived with
my parents But that s all.

Q. 고국을 떠나기로 한 이후로 다녀온 적이 있나요?

A. 아니요. 나온 이후 고향에 다시 가 본 적이 없습니다. 만나고 싶은 사람이 없어요.
가끔 부모님과 함께 살던 고향이 그리울 때가 있지만, 그게 전부예요.

Have you been to your country since you left?

No, I haven't been my own country since I left. There is no one I want to meet. Sometimes I miss my hometown where I lived with my parents. But that's all.

Q. 고국을 떠나기로 한 이후로 다녀온 적이 있나요?

A. 아니요. 나온 이후 고향에 다시 가 본 적이 없습니다. 만나고 싶은 사람이 없어요. 가끔 부모님과 함께 살던 고향이 그리울 때가 있지만, 그게 전부예요.

What was your impression of the UK?

I came here nobody was interested about me, but almost people stared at me because there was few of Asian people at the time

Q. 영국에 대한 인상은 어땠나요?

A. 여기에 왔을 때 아무도 저에게 관심을 가지지 않았어요. 하지만 당시에는 아시아 사람이 거의 없었기 때문에 거의 모든 사람들이 저를 쳐다봤어요.

What was your impression of the UK?

I came here nobody was interested about me, but almost people stared at me because there was few of Asian people at the time.

Q. 영국에 대한 인상은 어땠나요?

A. 여기에 왔을 때 아무도 저에게 관심을 가지지 않았어요. 하지만 당시에는 아시아 사람이 거의 없었기 때문에 거의 모든 사람들이 저를 쳐다봤어요.

What did and do you do for a living?

I used to do everything I was able to do and now I teach children at a church

Q. 생계유지를 위해 무엇을 했고, 현재는 무엇을 하고 있나요?

A. 과거에는 할 수 있는 모든 일을 했고, 지금은 교회에서 아이들을 가르치고 있습니다.

What did and
do you do for a living?

I used to do everything I was able to do and now I teach children at a church.

Q. 생계유지를 위해 무엇을 했고, 현재는 무엇을 하고 있나요?

A. 과거에는 할 수 있는 모든 일을 했고, 지금은 교회에서 아이들을 가르치고 있습니다.

18
18
18 18 18
lee3
18
Lee

Have you met any people to report or ask for help with your state?

I don't think I have

Q. 당신을 신고하거나, 당신이 도움을 요청하기 위해 만난 사람이 있나요?

A. 그런 사람은 만난 적이 없는 것 같아요.

Have you met any people to report or ask for help with your state?

I don't think I have

Q. 당신을 신고하거나, 당신이 도움을 요청하기 위해 만난 사람이 있나요?

A. 그런 사람을 만난 적이 없는 것 같아요.

Have you confessed to or
talked to anyone about your illegal situation?

yes,
i've told a priest my past,
why I came here,
because I was
sufferedbythe fact.
He seemed to
understand

Q. 불법 체류에 대해 고백하거나 누군가와 이야기한 적이 있나요?

A. 네, 저의 과거와 제가 왜 여기에 왔는지, 그 사실 때문에 고통받았던 것을
한 신부님께 말씀드렸습니다. 그분은 이해하는 것 같았어요.

Have you confessed to or
talked to anyone about your illegal situation?

yes,
I've told a priest my past
why I came here,
because I was
suffered with the fact,
He seemed to
understand

Q. 불법 체류에 대해 고백하거나 누군가와 이야기한 적이 있나요?

A. 네, 저의 과거와 제가 왜 여기에 왔는지, 그 사실 때문에 고통받았던 것을 한 신부님께 말씀드렸습니다. 그분은 이해하는 것 같았어요.

What made you decide to leave your own country?

I'd lost my daughter
by mistake and
then i was divorced
without any alimony
I felt as if all the
people blamed me
so ididn't want to
live there

Q. 고국을 떠나기로 한 이유는 무엇인가요?

A. 실수로 딸을 잃었고, 그 후 양육비 없이 이혼했습니다. 모든 사람들이 저를 비난하는 것 같았어요. 거기에서 더 이상 살고 싶지 않았어요.

What made you decide to leave your own country?

I'd lost my daughter
by mistake and
then I was divorced
without any allowance
I felt as if all the
people blamed me
so I didn't want to
live there

Q. 고국을 떠나기로 한 이유는 무엇인가요?

A. 실수로 딸을 잃었고, 그 후 양육비 없이 이혼했습니다. 모든 사람들이 저를 비난하는 것 같았어요. 거기에서 더 이상 살고 싶지 않았어요.

What are the most significant differences between being legal and illegal?

It is big and
small differences
my thought about
being the UK
Actually,
nothings were
changed
around me
since
I've got ill.

Q. 합법 체류와 불법 체류 사이의 가장 큰 차이점은 무엇인지요?

A. 합법과 불법 체류에 대한 제 생각에는 크고 작은 차이가 있습니다.
실제로 주변은 아무것도 달라진 것은 없었습니다. 이후 병을 얻기도 했어요.

What are the most significant differences between being legal and illegal?

It is big and
small differences
my thought about
being legal and
illegal
nothing were
changed
around me
since
I've got ill

Q. 합법 체류와 불법 체류 사이의 가장 큰 차이점은 무엇인가요?

A. 합법과 불법 체류에 대한 제 생각에는 크고 작은 차이가 있습니다.
실제로 주변은 아무것도 달라진 것은 없었습니다. 이후 병을 얻기도 했어요.

If you were able to go back to the time when you made the decision to come here illegally, would you make the same choice?

I m not sure
but I would make the
same decision leaving
my contry.
because I remember
how much I suffered
and was painful my past

However, I sometimes imagine
if I lived there
I would've been better?

Q. 당신이 이곳에 불법 체류를 결정했던 시점으로 돌아갈 수 있다면, 같은 선택을 하겠습니까?

A. 확실하지 않아요. 하지만 내 나라를 떠나기로 한 결정은 다시 할 것 같습니다. 제가 얼마나 고통받았는지, 과거가 얼마나 아팠는지 기억하기 때문입니다. 그러나 가끔, 제가 거기에 살았다면 괜찮았을까 상상하기도 합니다.

If you were able to go back to the time when you made the decision to come here illegally, would you make the same choice?

I'm not sure
that I would make the
same decision leaving
my country
because I remember
how much I suffered
and was painful my past

— however I couldn't imagine
if I lived there
I would've been what?

Q. 당신이 이곳에 불법 체류를 결정했던 시점으로 돌아갈 수 있다면, 같은 선택을 하겠습니까?

A. 확실하지 않아요. 하지만 제 나라를 떠나기로 한 결정은 다시 할 것 같습니다. 제가 얼마나 고통받았는지, 과거가 얼마나 아팠는지 기억하기 때문입니다. 그러나 가끔, 제가 거기에 살았다면 괜찮았을까 상상하기도 합니다.

If you know someone, especially refugees or asylum seekers, who is considering using the '14-year rule' or contemplating living illegally in the UK, would you offer them any advice or recommendations?

I don't want to
recommend people to
live illegally in anywhere
although I did
I know how much
it is painful
than their thoughts

Q. 만약 당신이 아는 난민이나 망명 신청자가 '14년 규정'을 염두에 두거나
영국에서 불법 체류를 고려하고 있다면, 그들에게 어떤 조언이나 추천을 하겠습니까?

A. 저는 어디에서든 불법으로 살라고 추천하고 싶지 않아요. 비록 제가 그랬더라도요.
이제 전 그런 삶이 사람들의 생각보다 훨씬 더 고통스럽다는 것을 알고 있습니다.

If you know someone, especially refugees or asylum seekers, who is considering using the '14-year rule' or contemplating living illegally in the UK, would you offer them any advice or recommendations?

Q. 만약 당신이 아는 난민이나 망명 신청자가 '14년 규정'을 염두에 두거나 영국에서 불법 체류를 고려하고 있다면, 그들에게 어떤 조언이나 추천을 하겠습니까?

A. 저는 어디에서든 불법으로 살라고 추천하고 싶지 않아요, 비록 제가 그랬더라도요. 이제 전 그런 삶이 사람들의 생각보다 훨씬 더 고통스럽다는 것을 알고 있습니다.

Northampton
91
95
110
London

What is it like to seek refuge or asylum while living illegally in the UK?

"prison"

Q. 영국에서 불법으로 피난처, 망명을 갈구하는 삶이란?

A. "감옥"

What is it like to seek refuge or asylum while living illegally in the UK?

Q. 영국에서 불법으로 피난처, 망명을 갈구하는 삶이란?

A. "감옥".

Do you recall what your initial action was as soon as you were granted 'ILR'?

I talked a policeman
I asked some
direction even though
I knew. It
was pretty funny.

Q 'ILR'을 부여받은 직후에 당신이 한 첫 번째 행동이 무엇인지 기억하나요?

A 경찰관에게 말을 걸었어요. 알고 있었음에도 불구하고 길을 물어봤죠. 꽤 웃겼어요.

Do you recall what your initial action was as soon as you were granted 'ILR'?

I talked a policeman
I asked some
direction even though
I knew. LOL
was pretty funny -

Q. 'ILR'을 부여받은 직후에 당신이 한 첫 번째 경험이 무엇인지 기억하나요?

A. 경찰관에게 말을 걸었어요. 알고 있었음에도 불구하고 길을 물어봤죠. 꽤 웃겼어요.

Do you have something that you always keep with you?

Yes, I usually keep a rosary which I bought for my daughter.

Q. 항상 가지고 다니는 물건이 있나요?

A. 네, 제 딸을 위해 구매한 묵주를 항상 가지고 다닙니다.

Do you have something that you always keep with you?

Q. 항상 가지고 다니는 물건이 있나요?

A. 네, 제 딸을 위해 구매한 묵주를 항상 가지고 다닙니다.

Yes, I usually keep a rosary which I bought for my daughter

Are you happy with how things are for you right now?

I don't know I haven't laughed loudly lately. I don't know. how I can be happy.

Q. 지금 당신의 현재 삶에 만족하고 있나요?

A. 모르겠어요. 최근에 크게 웃어 본 적이 없어요.
어떻게 행복할 수 있는지 모르겠어요.

Are you happy with how things are for you right now?

I don't know. I haven't laughed loudly lately. I don't know how I can be happy

Q. 지금 당신의 현재 삶에 만족하고 있나요?

A. 모르겠어요, 최근에 크게 웃어 본 적이 없어요.
어떻게 행복할 수 있는지 모르겠어요.

EVERYONE HAS THE RIGHT FREEDOM OF PEACEFUL ASSEMBLY AND TO FREEDOM OF ASSOCIATION WITH OTHERS INCLUDING THE RIGHT TO FORM AND TO JOIN TRADE UNIONS FOR THE PROTECTION OF HIS INTERESTS.

모든 사람은 평화적 집회의 자유와 다른 사람들과 결사의 자유를 가질 권리가 있다. 이에는 자신의 이익을 보호하기 위해 노동조합을 결성하고 가입할 권리가 포함된다. — 유럽인권협약 제11조

Article 11 — European Convention on Human Rights

EVERYONE HAS

FREEDOM OF
PEACEFUL ASSEMBLY
AND TO FREEDOM
OF ASSOCIATION WITH
OTHERS INCLUDING
THE RIGHT TO FORM
AND

#2
ANONYMOUS

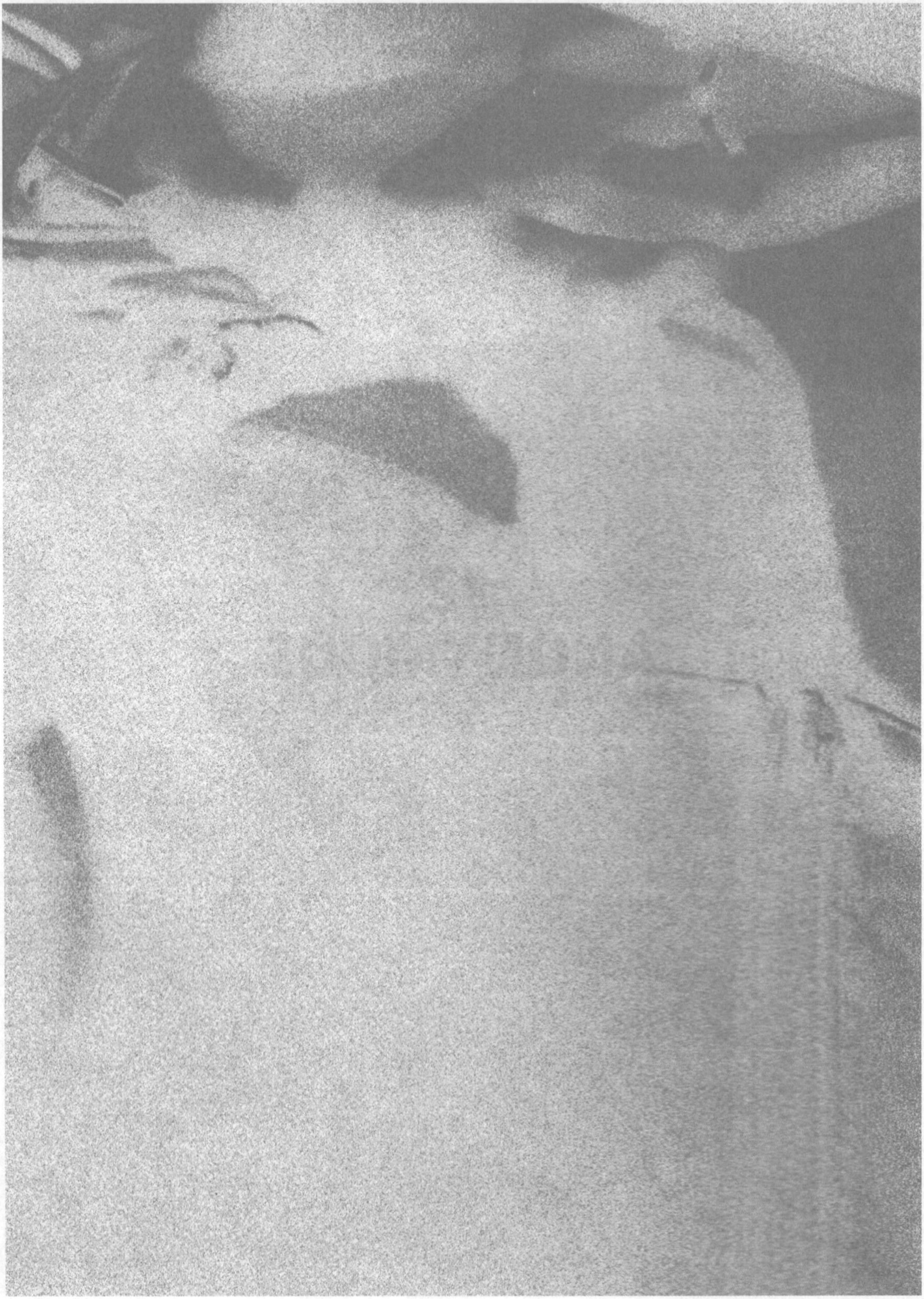

Please
introduce yourself.

My name is [redacted].

I 'am . [redacted]-year-old.

I come from [redacted].

Q. 자기소개 부탁드립니다.

A. 제 이름은 -입니다. 전 -살이고 -에서 왔어요.

Please
introduce yourself.

Q. 자기소개 부탁드립니다.

A. 제 이름은 -입니다. 전 -살이고 -에서 왔어요.

How long did it take for you to be granted indefinite leave to remain?

15 years

How long did it take for you to be granted indefinite leave to remain?

How long did it take for you to be granted 'indefinite leave to remain'?

Q. 영구 체류 자격을 받기까지 얼마나 걸렸나요?

A. 15년.

Have you been to your country since you left?

No, it was impossible to go back to [redacted]. I haven't seen my mama for 8 years. When my mama came here to see me in 2008, she started to weep uncontrollably and she didn't let go her hold of my hands until she left.

Have you been to
your country since you left?

Q. 고국을 떠나기로 한 이후로 다녀온 적이 있나요?

A. 아니요, 거기로 돌아가는 것은 불가능했습니다. 8년 동안 엄마를 못 봤어요. 2008년에 엄마가 저를 보러 여기에 왔을 때, 엄마는 계속 울었고, 떠날 때까지 제 손을 놓지 않았어요.

What was your impression of the UK?

if I look back on the 15 years, everything is too fast and changeable in the UK. There if I look back is no enough time to get used to something for me. Especially Immigrants now used to be easy to study but recently it is, I don't think so.

Q. 영국에 대한 인상은 어땠나요

A. 지난 15년을 돌아보면, 영국의 모든 것은 너무 빠르고 변화무쌍해요. 특히 이민자들에게 예전에는 공부가 쉬웠을지 몰라도, 최근에는 그렇지 않다고 생각합니다.

What was your impression of the UK?

Q. 영국에 대한 인상은 어땠나요?

A. 지난 15년을 돌아보면, 영국의 모든 것은 너무 빠르고 변화무쌍해요. 특히 이민자들에게 예전에는 공부가 쉬웠을지 몰라도, 최근에는 그렇지 않다고 생각합니다.

What did and
do you do for a living?

I had focused on only studying when I had been legal, however I used to work at [redacted] and fruit and vegetable stores at night since I lost the visa.

Oh, I'am a vegetarian.

What did and do you do for a living?

Q. 생계유지를 위해 무엇을 했고, 현재는 무엇을 하고 있나요?

A. 합법적이었을 때는 공부에만 집중했지만, 비자를 잃은 이후로는 밤에 과일과 채소 가게에서 일했습니다. 아, 저는 채식주의자입니다.

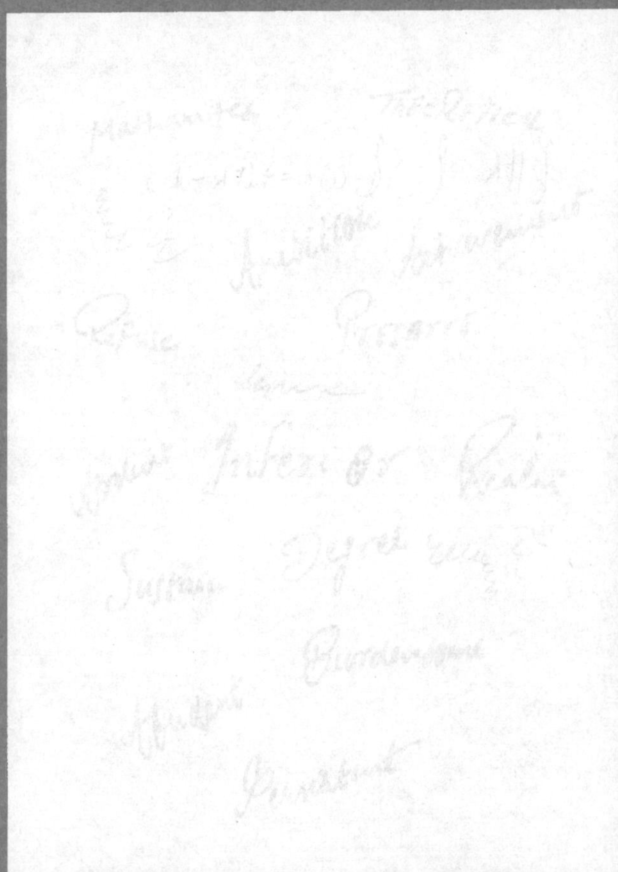

Mathematics Theoretical

[illegible]

Nutrition Achievement

Refuse Preserve

Famous Inferior Realm

Sustain Degree

Burdensome

Abundant

Persistent

What was the most memorable experience during your time living in the UK illegally?

I have been afraid of daytime. I Couldn't expect I would become one of illegal immigrants. I thought going out during daytime was extremely dangerous so, I went out only at night for few of years. My landlady thought I was very strange and asked a lot of things what I was doing and my job was. I felt uneasy due to her eyes. so I moved out of that house. if I had been forcibly repatriated, I had have had a marriage of convenience for my family. However I realized nobody was interested in me and then I took action normally.

Q. 영국에서 불법으로 생활하는 동안 가장 기억에 남는 경험은 무엇이었나요?

A. 낮이 무서웠어요. 제가 불법 이민자가 될 줄은 상상도 못 했거든요. 그래서 몇 년 동안은 밤에만 외출했어요. 집주인은 제가 이상한 사람이라고 생각했고, 저에 대해 많은 것을 물어봤어요. 그 눈초리가 불편해 결국 그 집을 나왔어요. 만약 강제로 추방당할 처지였다면 가족을 위해 결혼을 했을 거예요. 하지만 사실 아무도 저에게 관심이 없었기 때문에, 저는 평범하게 행동하기 시작했어요.

What was the most memorable experience during your time living in the UK illegally?

I have been afraid of daytime. I couldn't expect I would become one of illegal immigrants. I thought going out during daytime was extremely dangerous so I went out only at night for few of years. My landlady thought I was very strange and asked a lot of things what I was doing and my business. I felt really sick to her. So I moved out of the house. If I had been forcibly deported, I had have had a marriage of convenience for my family. However, I realized nobody was interested in me and then I started acting normally.

Q. 영국에서 불법으로 생활하는 동안 가장 기억에 남는 경험은 무엇이었나요?

A. 낮이 무서웠어요. 제가 불법 이민자가 될 줄은 상상도 못 했거든요. 그래서 몇 년 동안은 밤에만 외출했어요. 집주인은 제가 이상한 사람이라고 생각했고, 저에 대해 많은 것을 물어봤어요. 그 눈초리가 불편해 결국 그 집을 나왔어요. 만약 강제로 추방당할 처지였다면 가족을 위해 결혼을 했을 거예요. 하지만 사실 아무도 저에게 관심이 없었기 때문에, 저는 평범하게 행동하기 시작했어요.

Have you confessed to or
talked to anyone about your illegal situation?

Yes, I have talked to my friend who was in the same situation. She talked to me first about her situation before she left to her own country. She was ambivalent about her illegal life it was going to be worth or worse at that time. To get some advise, she told me and then I told her my life as a friend.

Q. 불법 체류에 대해 고백하거나 누군가와 이야기한 적이 있나요?

A. 네. 같은 상황에 있던 친구에게 말했습니다. 그녀가 고국으로 돌아가기 전에 먼저 자신의 상황에 대해 저에게 털어놓았습니다. 그녀의 불법 체류 상황이 가치가 있는 것인지, 더 나빠질지에 대해 고민이 많아 조언을 구하기 위해서요. 저도 친구로서 제 삶에 대해 그녀에게 말했습니다.

Have you confessed to or talked to anyone about your illegal situation?

Q. 불법 체류에 대해 고백하거나 누군가와 이야기한 적이 있나요?

A. 네, 같은 상황에 있던 친구에게 말했습니다. 그녀가 고국으로 돌아가기 전에 먼저 자신의 상황에 대해 저에게 털어놓았습니다. 그녀의 불법 체류 상황이 가치가 있는 것인지, 더 나빠질지에 대해 고민이 많아 조언을 구하기 위해서요. 저도 친구로서 제 삶에 대해 그녀에게 말했습니다.

What made you decide to leave your own country?

I had heard there would be more a lot of Opportunities than my Country [redacted] to get job in my field, Mathematics.

What made you decide to
leave your own country?

Q. 고국을 떠나기로 한 이유는 무엇인가요?

A. 제 전공인 수학 관련 일자리를 찾는 것이 고국보다 여기가 훨씬 더 기회가 많다고 해서요.

What are the most significant differences between being legal and illegal?

I think I don't have to worry a study on legal remedy and I am able to carry on learning as much as I can and I can meet with my mama at anytime.

Q. 합법 체류와 불법 체류 사이의 가장 큰 차이점은 무엇인가요?

A. 법적 구제에 대한 걱정을 하지 않아도 되고, 원하는 만큼 배울 수 있으며, 언제든지 엄마를 만날 수 있다는 것이죠.

What are the most significant differences between being legal and illegal?

Q. 합법 체류와 불법 체류 사이의 가장 큰 차이점은 무엇인가요?

A. 법적 구제에 대한 걱정을 하지 않아도 되고, 원하는 만큼 배울 수 있으며, 언제든지 엄마를 만날 수 있다는 것이죠.

If you were able to go back to the time when you made the decision to come here illegally, would you make the same choice?

if I was able to keep this memory
I would make different choice. Such
as staying in [redacted] or going to the
USA. But I now know the illegal life

If you were able to go back to the time when you made the decision to come here illegally, would you make the same choice?

Q. 당신이 이곳에 불법 체류를 결정했던 시점으로 돌아갈 수 있다면, 같은 선택을 하겠습니까?

A. 지난 기억을 유지한 채 돌아갈 수 있다면, 다른 선택을 하겠습니다. 예를 들어, -에 머무르거나 미국으로 가는 것과 같은 선택 말이죠. 저는 불법의 삶이란 어떤 것인지 알고 있어요.

If you know someone, especially refugees or asylum seekers, who is considering using the '14-year rule' or contemplating living illegally in the UK, would you offer them any advice or recommendations?

This is not easy giving or recommending it to someone. Also I heard the 14-year rule will be tightened and chopped. That means the Person will be more Painful to endure such the long Period. I am Still not Sure Sacrifice of my youth is worth? or not?

I don't want to recommend it.

No, not everyone can do this.

Q. 만약 당신이 아는 난민이나 망명 신청자가 '14년 규정'을 염두에 두거나 영국에서 불법 체류를 고려하고 있다면, 그들에게 어떤 조언이나 추천을 하겠습니까?

A. 이건 쉽게 추천하거나 권할 수 있는 게 아니에요. 또, 14년 규정이 더 엄격해진다는 이야기를 들었어요. 그 말은, 그 기간을 견디는 게 더 힘들어진다는 것이겠죠. 저도 아직 내 청춘을 희생한 게 가치가 있었는지 확신이 안 서기 때문에 추천하고 싶지 않아요. 이건 누구나 할 수 있는 게 아니니까요.

If you know someone, especially refugees or asylum seekers, who is considering using the '14-year rule' or contemplating living illegally in the UK, would you offer them any advice or recommendations?

This is not easy giving or recommending
to other someone. Also I heard the 14-year
rule will be tightened and complex
it means because the person will be more
painful to endure such the long period
I am still not sure sacrifice of my
youth was worth it or not.

I don't want to recommend this
It's not everyone can do this.

Q. 만약 당신이 아는 난민이나 망명 신청자가 '14년 규정'을 염두에 두거나 영국에서 불법 체류를 고려하고 있다면, 그들에게 어떤 조언이나 추천을 하겠습니까?

A. 이건 쉽게 추천하거나 권할 수 있는 게 아니에요. 또, 14년 규정이 더 엄격해진다는 이야기를 들었어요. 그 말은, 그 기간을 견디는 게 더 힘들어진다는 것이겠죠. 저도 아직 내 청춘을 희생한 게 가치가 있었는지 확신이 안 서기 때문에 추천하고 싶지 않아요. 이건 누구나 할 수 있는 게 아니니까요.

(I - λT)f = 0
C0([0,1])

Do you recall what your initial action was as soon as you were granted 'ILR'?

As I remember, it was night. I couldn't believe the letter was mine. I went out and ran around all over the town with the letter as soon as I checked it was mine. Maybe, if someone saw me he would think I was insane.

Q. 'ILR'을 부여받은 직후에 당신이 한 첫 번째 경험이 무엇인지 기억하나요?

A. 밤이었던 걸로 기억해요. 그 서류가 제 것이라는 것을 믿을 수 없었어요. 제 것이라는 것을 확인하자마자 밖으로 나가서 동네를 뛰어다녔어요. 누군가가 저를 봤다면, 저를 미친 사람으로 생각했을 거예요.

Do you recall what your initial action was as soon as you were granted 'ILR'?

Q. 'ILR'을 부여받은 직후에 당신이 한 첫 번째 행동이 무엇인지 기억하나요?

A. 밤이었던 걸로 기억해요. 그 서류가 제 것이라는 것을 믿을 수 없었어요. 제 것이라는 것을 확인하자마자 밖으로 나가서 동네를 뛰어다녔어요. 누군가가 저를 봤다면, 저를 미친 사람으로 생각했을 거예요.

Do you have something that
you always keep with you?

Yes, but not special, I always bring
a mathmatical formula to solve the
answer anytime. it makes me concentrate
and comfortable. When I am solving
such a complicated mathematics reminds
of why I am here.

Q. 항상 가지고 다니는 물건이 있나요?

A. 네, 특별하지는 않지만, 언제든지 해답을 찾을 수 있는 수학 공식을 항상 가지고 다녀요. 이것은 저를 집중시키고 편안하게 해 주죠. 복잡한 수학 문제를 푸는 것은 스스로에게 내가 왜 여기에 있는지를 상기시켜 줍니다.

Do you have something that you always keep with you?

Yes, not special. I always carry a mathematical formula to solve the answer anytime - it makes me concentrate and comfortable. When I am solving into a complicated mathematics, reminds of why I am here.

Q. 항상 가지고 다니는 물건이 있나요?

A. 네, 특별하지는 않지만, 언제든지 해답을 찾을 수 있는 수학 공식을 항상 가지고 다녀요. 이것은 저를 집중시키고 편안하게 해 주죠. 복잡한 수학 문제를 푸는 것은 스스로에게 내가 왜 여기에 있는지를 상기시켜 줍니다.

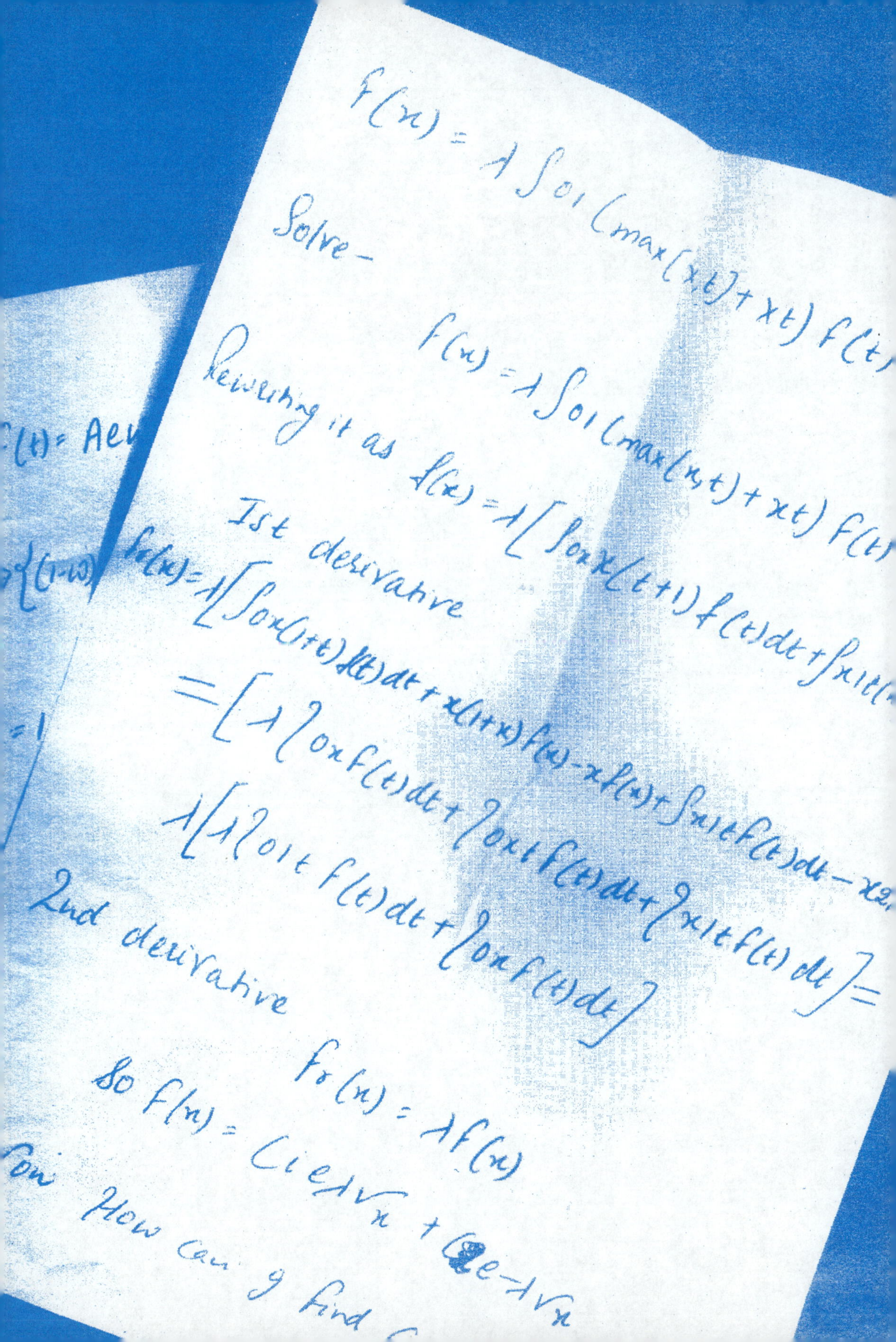
f(x) = λ ∫01 (max(x,t) + xt) f(t
Solve-
f(x) = λ ∫01 (max(x,t) + xt) f(t)
Rewriting it as f(x) = λ[∫0x (t+1) f(t)dt + ∫x1 t(
1st derivative
f'(x) = λ[∫0x (1+t) f(t)dt + x(1+x)f(x) - xf(x) + ∫x1 t f(t)dt - x
= [λ ∫0x f(t)dt + ∫0x t f(t)dt + ∫x1 t f(t) dt] =
λ[λ ∫01 t f(t)dt + ∫0x f(t)dt]
2nd derivative
f''(x) = λf(x)
So f(x) = C1 eλ√x + C2 e-λ√x
How can I find
f(t) = Ae

Are you happy with
how things are for you right now?

To be honest, I am not. I feel regretful over my vanished youth. But, what can I do? it is irremediable. That was my choice. I am enjoying my life although it is terrible. I must be doing something to be happy.

Q. 지금 당신의 현재 삶에 만족하시나요?

A. 솔직히 말하자면 만족하지 않아요. 잃어버린 젊음에 대해 후회하고 있어요. 하지만 제가 할 수 있는 게 뭐 있나요? 이제 다시 돌이킬 수 없어요. 제 선택이었으니까요. 비록 끔찍하더라도 저는 제 삶을 즐기고 있어요. 행복해지기 위해서는 뭔가를 해야만 하니까요.

Are you happy with how things are for you right now?

Q. 지금 당신의 현재 삶에 만족하고 있나요?

A. 솔직히 말하자면, 만족하지 않아요. 잃어버린 젊음에 대해 후회하고 있어요. 하지만 제가 할 수 있는 게 무엇이겠어요? 다시 돌이킬 수 없어요. 제 선택이었으니까요. 비록 끔찍하더라도, 저는 제 삶을 즐기고 있어요. 행복해지기 위해서는 뭔가를 해야만 하니까요.

EVERY NATURAL OR LEGAL PERSON IS **ENTITLED TO THE PEACEFUL ENJOYMENT OF HIS POSSESSIONS.**

● 모든 자연인 또는 법인은 자신의 재산을 평화롭게 누릴 권리를 가진다. — 유럽인권협약 제1조

Article 1 — European Convention on Human Rights

EVERY NATURAL OR LEGAL PERSON IS

#3
ANONYMOUS

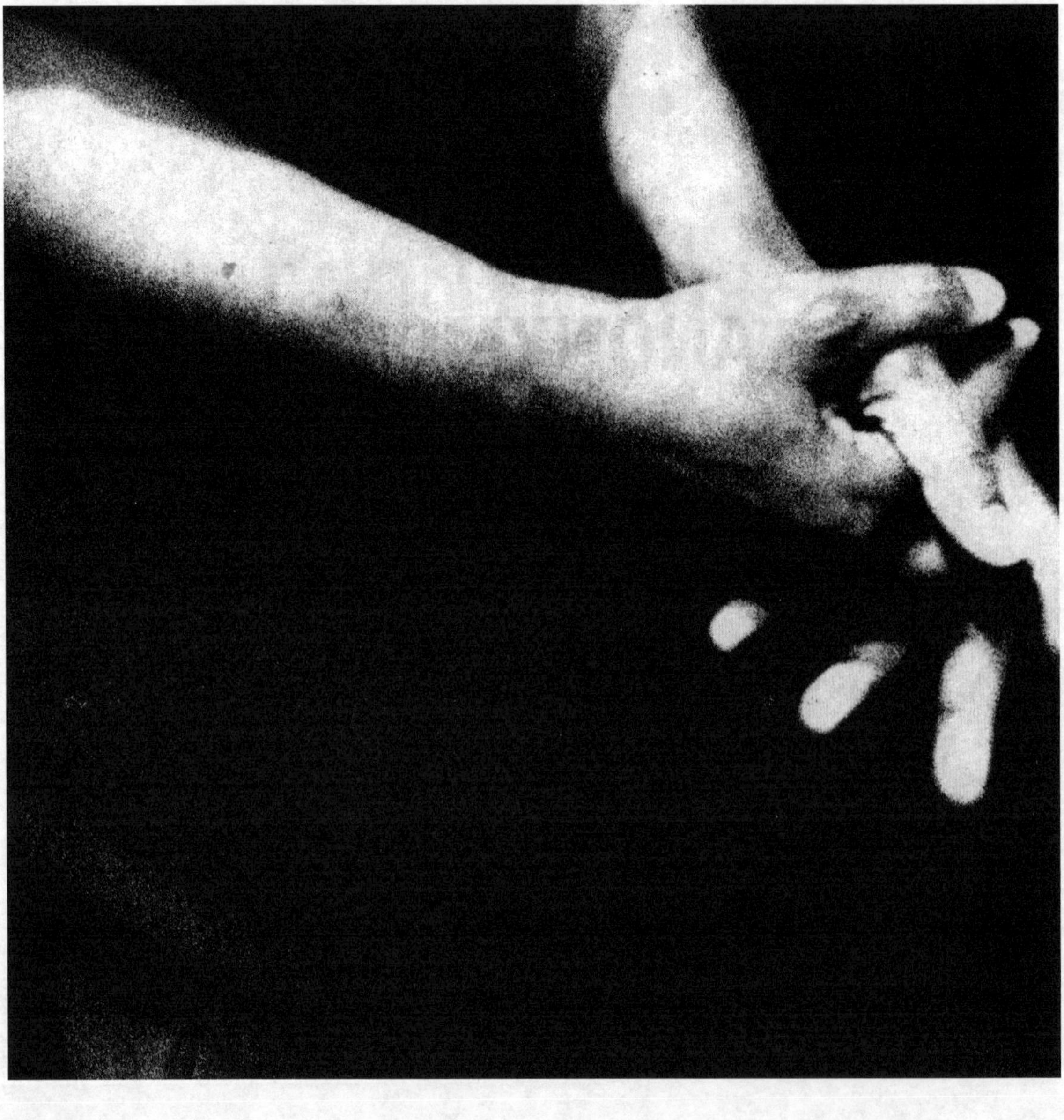

Please
introduce yourself.

Q. 자기소개 부탁드립니다.

A. 제 이름은 니샤드입니다. 저는 56살입니다. 그리고 방글라데시에서 왔습니다.

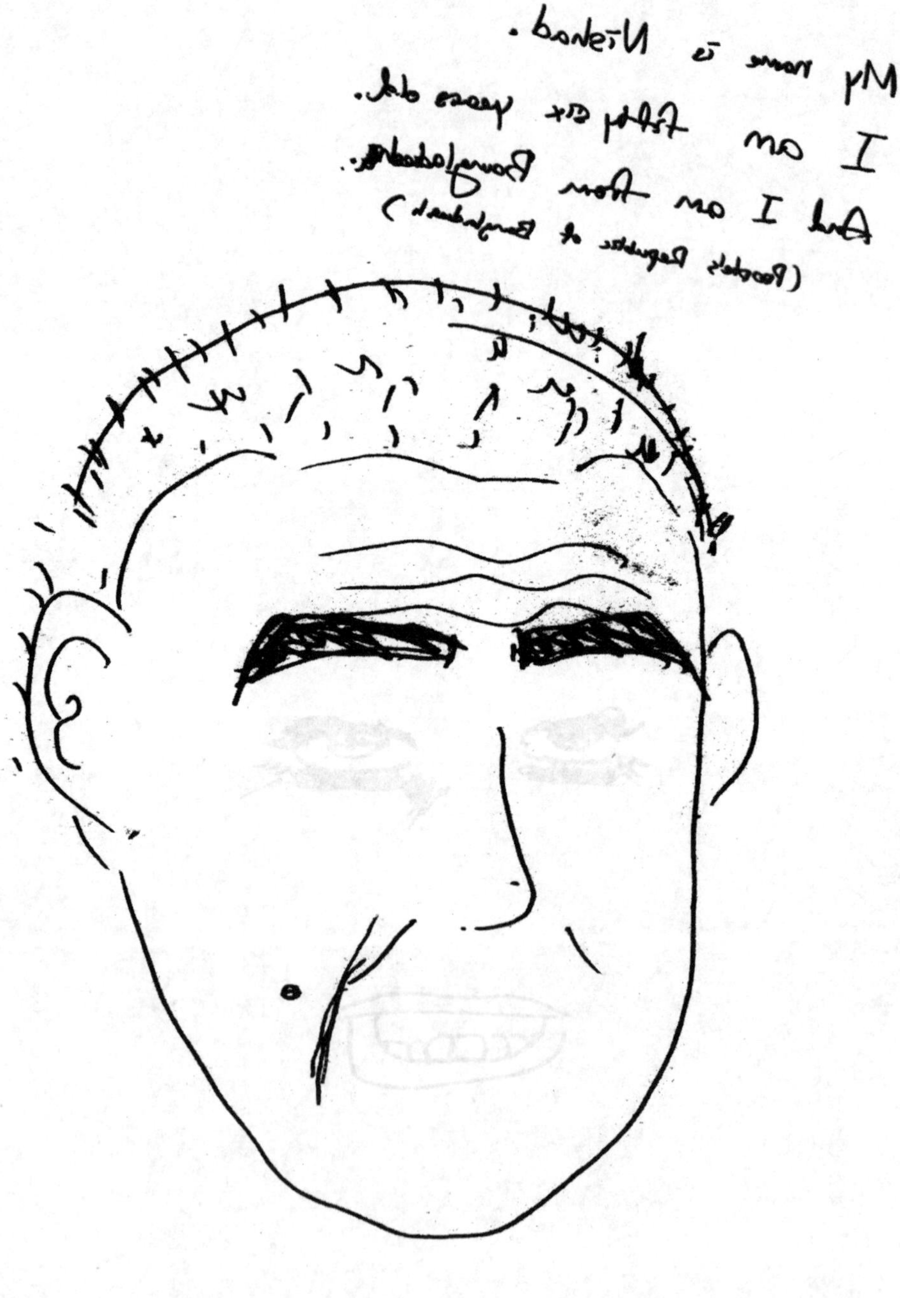
My name is Nishad.
I am fifty six years old.
And I am from Bangladesh.
(People's Republic of Bangladesh)

How long did it take for you to be granted 'indefinite leave to remain'?

It took me 14 years to get
'indefinite leave to remai...'

Q. 14년 체류 규정을 받기까지 얼마나 걸렸나요?

A. 14년 걸렸습니다.

It took me 14 years to get 'indefinite leave to remain'.

What did and do you do for a living?

I have done so many things such as
window cleaning, house
cleaning, waitress and taking care
of kids. Hard thing was that
as an illegally staying person
I couldn't complain even though
I got low paid. Eventually, I met
a nice person who is my
boss now so I am working for him
as a window cleaner

Q. 생계유지를 위해 무엇을 했고, 현재는 무엇을 하고 있나요?

A. 창문 청소, 집 청소, 웨이트리스, 아이들 돌보기 등 많은 일을 했습니다. 불법으로 체류하면서 힘든 점은 저임금을 받아도 불만을 제기할 수 없었다는 것입니다. 지금은 좋은 사장님을 만나 창문 청소 일을 하고 있습니다.

What did and
do you do for a living?

I have done so many things such as
window cleaning, house
cleaning, waitress, and taking care
of kids. Hard thing was that
as an illegally staying person
I couldn't complain even though
I got low paid. Eventually, I met
a nice person who is my
boss now so I am working for him
as a window cleaner.

Q. 생계유지를 위해 무엇을 했고, 현재는 무엇을 하고 있나요?

A. 창문 청소, 집 청소, 웨이트리스, 아이를 돌보기 등 많은 일을 했습니다. 불법으로 체류하면서 힘든 점은 저임금을 받아도 불만을 제기할 수 없었다는 것입니다. 지금은 좋은 사장님을 만나 창문 청소 일을 하고 있습니다.

What made you decide to leave your own country?

I came to UK to stud English first
As English is originated
from UK so I chose to come here.
I became to love UK
UK so I am here now

Q. 고국을 떠나기로 한 이유는 무엇인가요?

A. 처음에는 영어를 공부하기 위해 영국에 왔습니다. 영어는 영국어이기 때문에요. 영국을 사랑하게 되어 지금까지 여기 있습니다. 영국을 사랑하게 되어 지금까지 여기에 있습니다.

What made you
decide to leave
your own country?

I came to UK to study English first
As English is originated
from UK so I chose to come here.
I became to love UK
UK so I am here now.

Q. 고국을 떠나기로 한 이유는 무엇인가요?

A. 처음에는 영어를 공부하기 위해 영국에 왔습니다. 영어는 영국어이기 때문에요. 영국을 사랑하게 되어 지금까지 여기 있습니다. 영국을 사랑하게 되어 지금까지 여기에 있습니다.

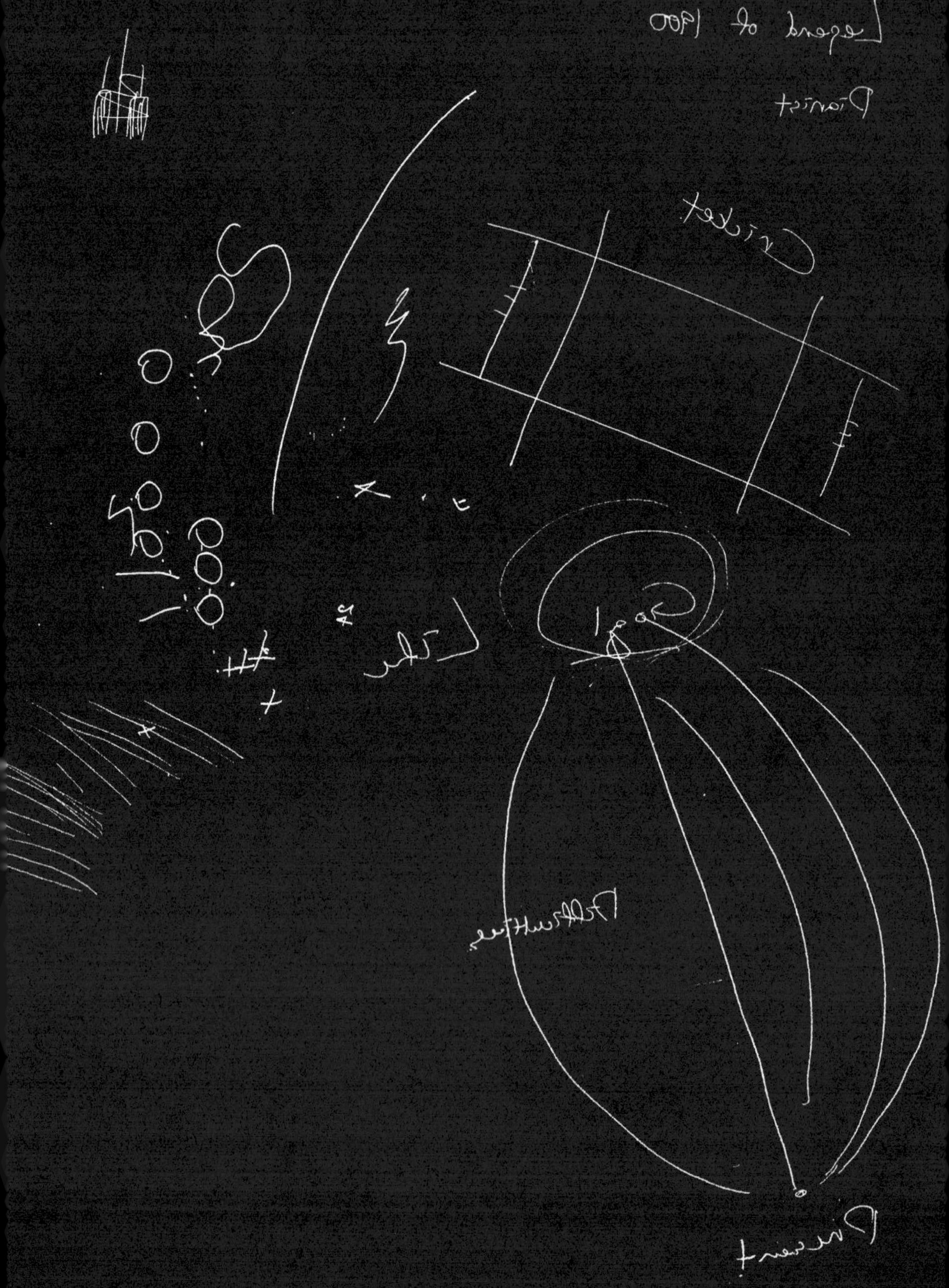
Legend of 1900
Pianist

What was the most memorable experience during your time living in the UK illegally?

Actually, there wasn't particularly good or bad memory

Q. 영국에서 불법으로 생활하는 동안 가장 기억에 남는 경험은 무엇인가요?

A. 사실 특별히 좋거나 나쁜 기억은 없습니다.

What was the most memorable experience during your time living in the UK illegally?

Actually, there wasn't particularly good or bad memory.

Q. 영국에서 불법으로 생활하는 동안 가장 기억에 남는 경험은 무엇인가요?

A. 사실 특별히 좋거나 나쁜 기억은 없습니다.

Have you been to your country since you left?

Just a couple of times
when I got a student visa.
I'm planning to visit my family soon

Q. 고국을 떠나기로 한 이후로 다시 다녀온 적이 있나요?

A. 학생 비자를 받았을 때 몇 번 다녀왔습니다. 곧 가족을 방문할 계획입니다.

Have you met any people to report or ask for help with your state?

I strongly believe that the secret can't be last long once it comes out of my mouth.
Now I got the granted visa
I'm telling you this

Q. 당신을 신고하거나, 당신이 도움을 요청하기 위해 만난 사람이 있나요?

A. 비밀은 오래가지 못한다고 강하게 믿습니다. 한 번 입 밖으로 나오면 말이죠. 이제 비자를 받았기 때문에 이렇게 말할 수 있어요.

Have you met any people to report or ask for help with your state?

I strongly believe that ~~Seree~~ ~~there~~ the secret can't ~~be~~ ~~any more~~ last long, once it comes out of my mouth. Now I got the guaranteed visa, I'm telling you this.

Q. 당신을 신고하거나, 당신이 도움을 요청하기 위해 만난 사람이 있나요?

A. 비밀은 오래가지 못한다고 강하게 믿습니다. 한 번 입 밖으로 나오면 말이죠. 이제 비자를 받았기 때문에 이렇게 말할 수 있어요.

If you were able to go back to the time when you made the decision to come here illegally, would you make the same choice?

I am not sure
about this.
However, What I am sure
about is that
I tend not to regret
about the past so.

Q. 당신이 이곳에 불법 체류를 결정했던 시점으로 돌아갈 수 있다면, 같은 선택을 하겠습니까?

A. 잘 모르겠어요. 하지만 확실한 것은 성격상 과거에 대해 후회하지 않아요.

I am not sure
about this.
However, What I am sure
about is that
I tend not to regret
about the past so.

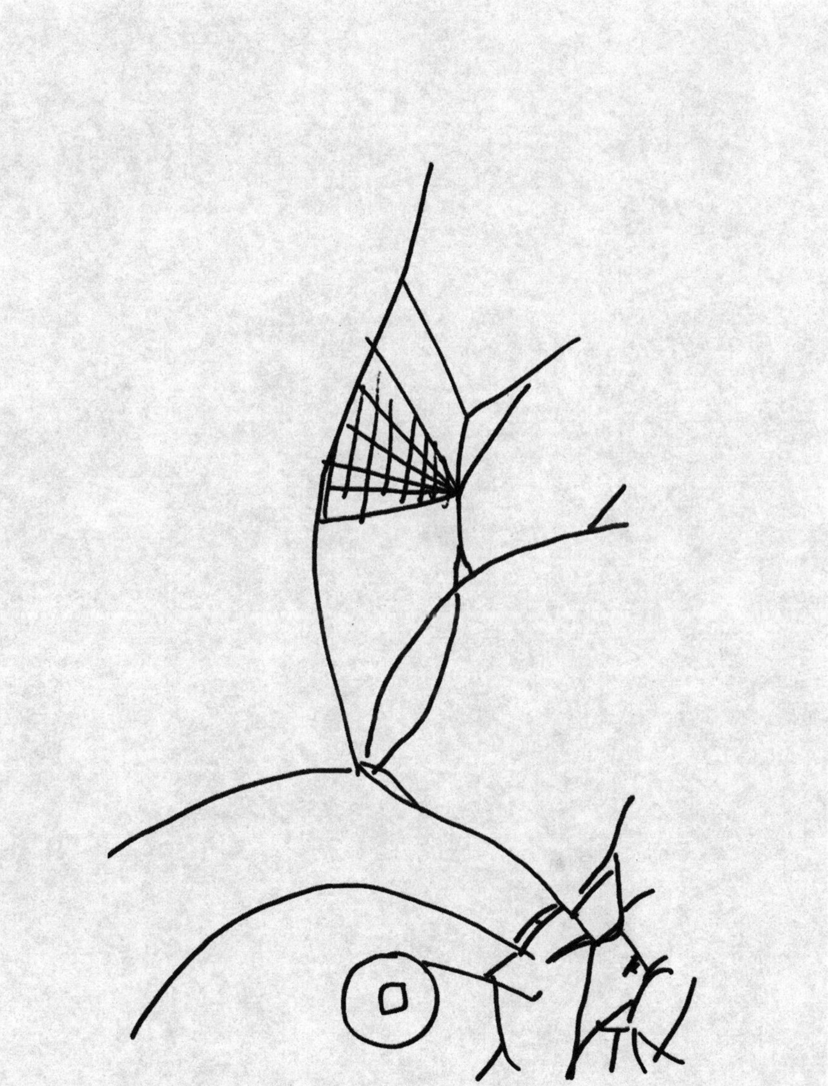

What are the most significant differences between being legal and illegal?

I stay where
I want to be.
Totally!

Q. 합법 체류와 불법 체류 사이의 가장 큰 차이점은 무엇인가요?

A. 제가 원하는 곳에 마음껏 머무를 수 있습니다. 완전히요!

What are the most significant differences between being legal and illegal?

I stay where
I want to be.
totally!

Q. 합법 체류와 불법 체류 사이의 가장 큰 차이점은 무엇인가요?

A. 제가 원하는 곳에 머물 수 있습니다, 완전히!

If you know someone, especially refugees or asylum seekers, who is considering using the '14-year rule' or contemplating living illegally in the UK, would you offer them any advice or recommendations?

Honestly, ~~[illegible]~~ I will not recommend to stay here illegally, however, I can't decide or I can't give any direction to someone how to live his or her life. It's entirely their decision to make because none will take responsibility for the consequences.

But there are always a way to stay legally so what I can tell them is that do not give up to get what you really want

Q. 만약 당신이 아는 난민이나 망명 신청자가 '14년 규정'을 염두에 두거나 영국에서 불법 체류를 고려하고 있다면, 그들에게 어떤 조언이나 추천을 하겠습니까?

A. 솔직히, 여기에서 불법으로 머무르라고 추천하진 않겠습니다. 하지만 제가 누군가의 삶에 대해 어떻게 살라고 하거나 방향을 제시할 수는 없습니다. 그것은 전적으로 그들의 결정이기 때문에, 결과에 대해서도 누구도 책임져 줄 수 없을 것입니다. 하지만 합법적으로 머무를 방법은 항상 있으므로 제가 그들에게 말할 수 있는 것은 정말 원하는 것을 얻기 위해 포기하지 말라는 것입니다.

If you know someone, especially refugees or asylum seekers, who is considering using the '14-year rule' or contemplating living illegally in the UK, would you offer them any advice or recommendations?

Honestly, I ~~will [illegible]~~. I will not recommend to stay here illegally, however, I can't decide or I can't give any direction to someone how to live his or her life. It's entirely their decision to make because noone will take responsibility for the consequences..

But there ~~are~~ always a way to stay legally so what I can tell them is that do not give up to get what you really want.

Q. 만약 당신이 아는 난민이나 망명 신청자가 '14년 규정'을 이용하거나 영국에서 불법 체류를 고려하고 있다면, 그들에게 어떤 조언이나 추천을 하겠습니까?

A. 솔직히, 여기에서 불법으로 머무르라고 추천하진 않겠습니다. 하지만 제가 누군가의 삶에 대해 어떻게 살라고 하거나 방향을 제시해 줄 수는 없습니다. 그것은 전적으로 그들의 결정이기 때문에, 결과에 대해서도 누구도 책임지지 않을 것입니다. 하지만 합법적으로 머무를 방법은 항상 있으므로 제가 그들에게 말할 수 있는 것은 정말 원하는 것을 얻기 위해 포기하지 말라는 것입니다.

Do you recall what your initial action was as soon as you were granted 'ILR'?

grabbing a beer
in a pub with folks
but I didn't tell them

Q. 'ILR'을 부여받은 직후에 당신이 한 첫 번째 경험이 무엇인지 기억하나요?

A. 친구들과 함께 펍에서 맥주를 마셨습니다. 하지만 친구들에게 이유를 말하진 않았어요.

Do you recall what your initial action was as soon as you were granted 'ILR'?

grabbing a beer
in a pub with folks.
But I didn't tell them

Q. 'ILR'을 부여받은 직후에 당신이 한 첫 번째 행동이 무엇인지 기억하나요?

A. 친구들과 함께 펍에서 맥주를 마셨습니다. 하지만 친구들에게 이유를 말하진 않았어요.

Do you have something that you always keep with you?

May be ... If I have one
it could be the things
that I've had for my UK life.
I just say that
I have many good memories.
Remembrance.

Q. 항상 가지고 다니는 물건이 있나요?

A. 아마도… 하나 있다면, 내 영국 생활 동안 가졌던 것들일 거예요. 그냥, 좋은 추억이 많이 있어요. 기억이요.

Do you have something that
you always keep with you?

Mary be ... If I have one
It could be the things
that I've had for my UK life.
I just say that
I have many good memories.
Remembrance.

Q 항상 가지고 다니는 물건이 있나요?

A 아마도… 하나 있다면 내 영국 생활 동안 가졌던 것들일 거예요. 그냥, 좋은 추억이 많이 있어요. 기억이요.

Are you happy with how things are for you right now?

I am happy now.
It doesn't have to be happier.
I am not greedy

Q. 지금 당신의 현재 삶에 만족하고 있나요?

A. 지금은 행복합니다. 더 행복할 필요는 없어요. 전 욕심이 많은 사람이 아니에요….

Are you happy with
how things are for you right now?

I am happy now.
It doesn't have to be happier.
I am not greedy.

Q. 지금 당신의 삶에 만족하고 있나요?
A. 지금은 행복합니다. 더 행복할 필요는 없어요. 전 욕심이 많은 사람이 아니에요…

EVERYONE HAS THE RIGHT TO LIFE, LIBERTY AND SECURITY OF PERSON.

모든 사람은 생명을 가질 권리, 자유를 누릴 권리, 자기 몸의 안전을 지킬 권리가 있다. — 세계인권선언 제3조

Article 3 — The Universal Declaration of Human Rights

EVERYONE HAS

AND SECURITY OF PERSON

#4 ANONYMOUS

네번째 인터뷰이는 인터뷰 이후 자신의 이야기를 공유하는 것에 대한 결정을 바꿔 자기가 쓴 글을 모두 지웠다.

All responses to the interviewee's writings were crossed out by herself because she changed her mind about sharing her story after the interview.

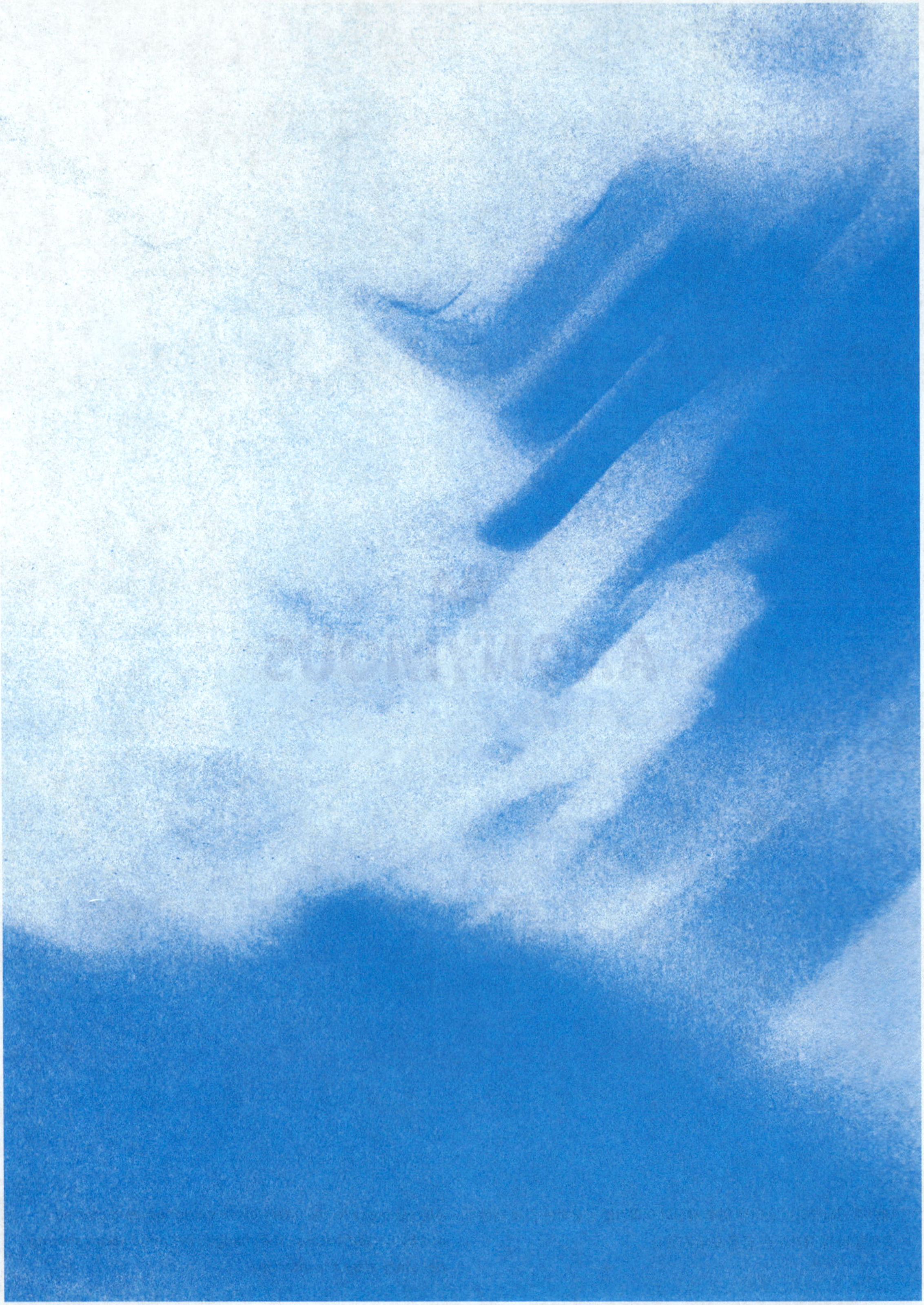

Please introduce yourself.

Q. 자기소개 부탁드립니다.

[redacted]

[redacted]

[redacted]

What did and do you do for a living?

Q. 생계유지를 위해 무엇을 했고, 현재는 무엇을 하고 있나요?

[redacted]

How long did it take for you to be granted 'indefinite leave to remain'?

Q. 14년 체류 규정을 받기까지 얼마나 걸렸나요?

[redacted]

What made you decide to leave your own country?

Q. 고국을 떠나기로 한 이유는 무엇인가요?

[redacted]

[redacted]

[redacted]

Why did you select the UK rather than another country?

Q. 왜 다른 나라 말고 영국을 선택했나요?

[redacted]

Have you been to your country since you left?

Q. 고국을 떠나기로 한 이후로 다시 다녀온 적이 있나요?

[redacted]

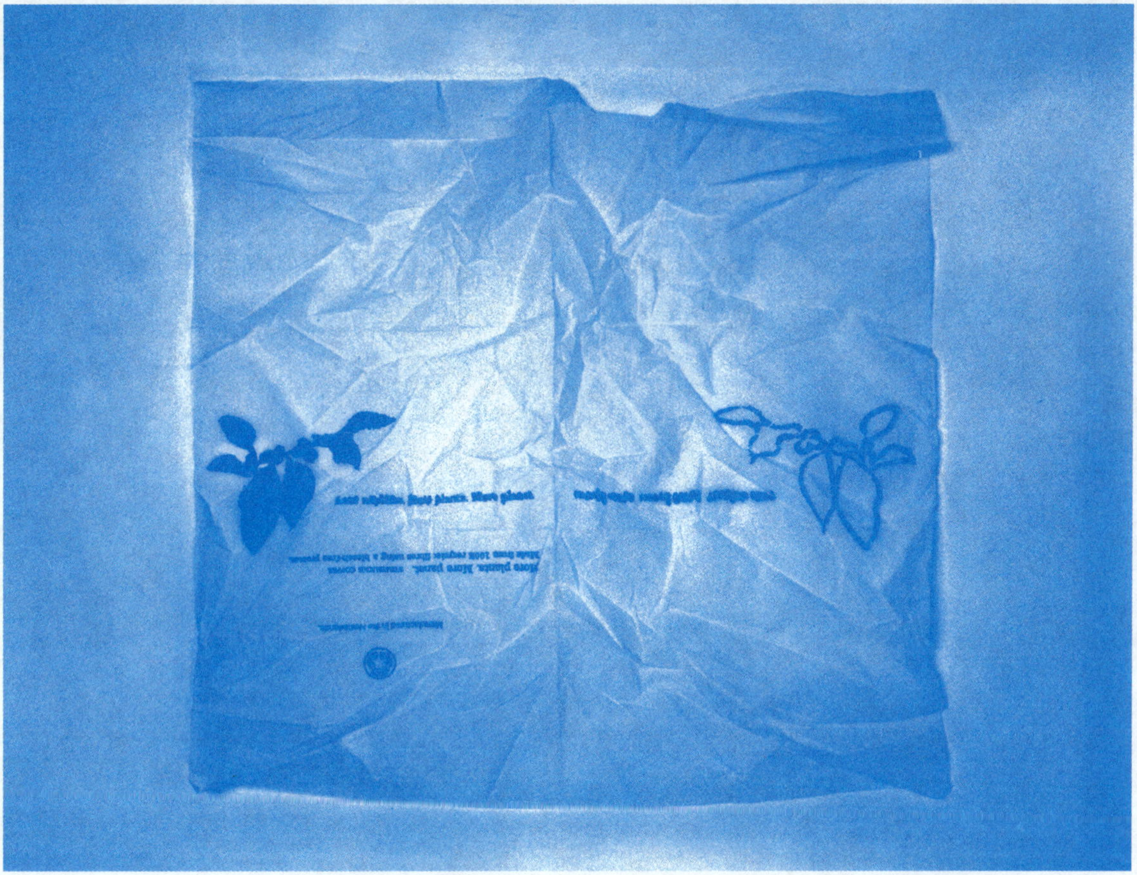

Less napkins. More plants. More planet.

What is your impression of the UK?

Q. 영국에 대한 인상은 어땠나요?

What were your thoughts when you were an illegal immigrant seeking refuge or asylum in the UK?

Q. 불법 이민자로서 피난처나 망명을 찾을 때 영국에서 어떤 생각을 했나요?

[redacted]

[redacted]

Have you confessed to or talked to anyone about your illegal situation?

Q. 불법 체류에 대해 고백하거나 누군가와 이야기한 적이 있나요?

What was the most memorable experience during your time living in the UK illegally?

Q. 영국에서 불법으로 생활하는 동안 가장 기억에 남는 경험은 무엇이었나요?

[redacted]

[redacted]

If you were able to go back to the time when you made the decision to come here illegally, would you make the same choice?

Q. 당신이 이곳에 불법 체류를 결정했던 시점으로 돌아갈 수 있다면, 같은 선택을 하겠습니까?

[redacted]

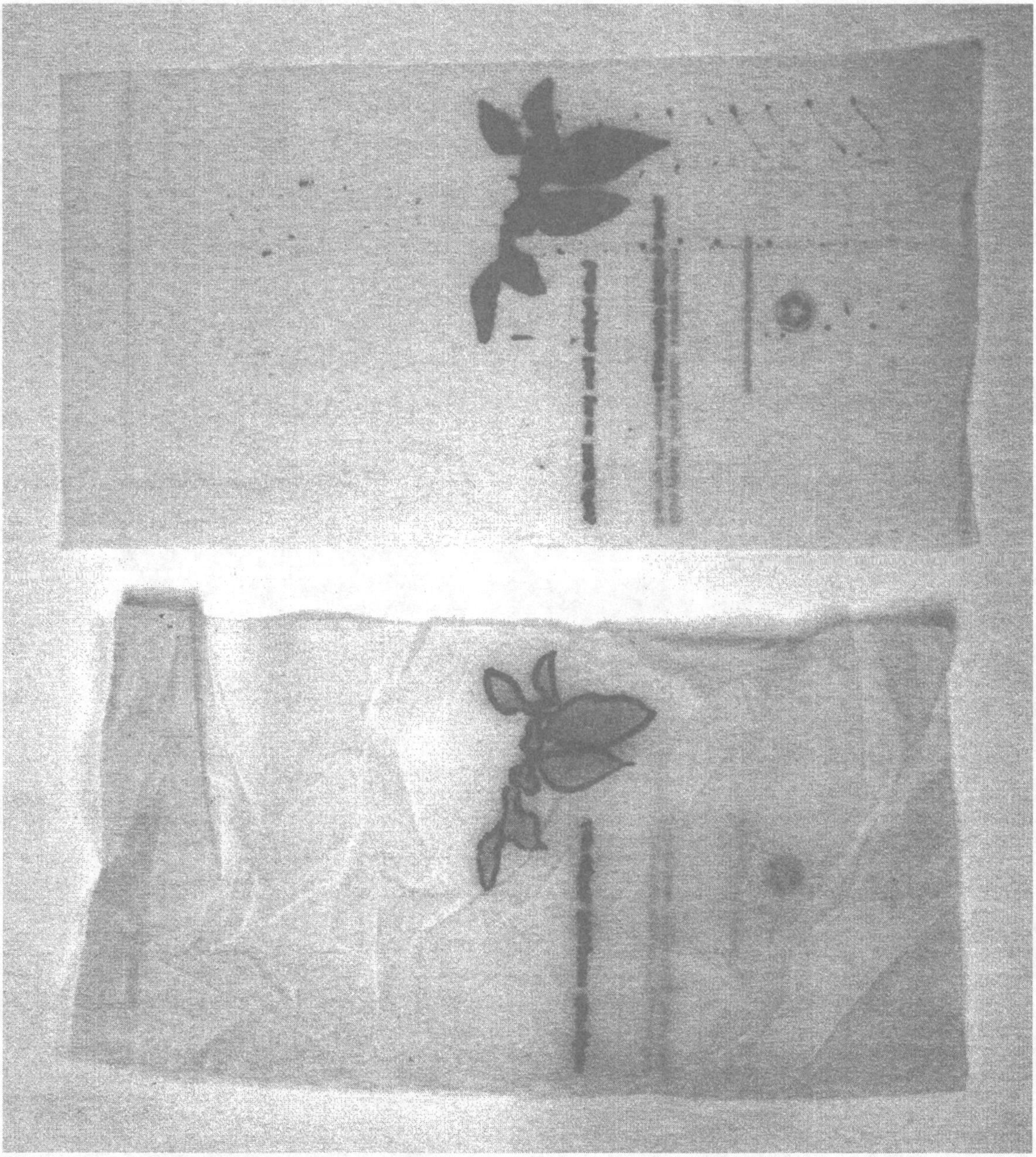

Do you recall what your initial action was as soon as you were granted 'ILR'?

Q. 'ILR'을 부여받은 직후에 당신이 한 첫 번째 경험이 무엇인지 기억하나요?

Do you have something that you always keep with you?

Q. 항상 가지고 다니는 물건이 있나요?

[redacted]

[redacted]

What are the most significant differences between being legal and illegal?

Q. 합법 체류와 불법 체류 사이의 가장 큰 차이점은 무엇인가요?

Are you happy with how things are for you right now?

Q. 지금 당신의 현재 삶에 만족하고 있나요?

[redacted]

[redacted]

THE HIGH CONTRACTING PARTIES SHALL SECURE TO

EVERYONE WITHIN THEIR JURISDICTION THE RIGHTS AND FREEDOMS.

협약 체결 당사국은 관할권 내 모든 사람의 권리와 자유를 보호해야 한다. — 유럽인권협약 제1조

Article 1 — The European Convention on Human Rights

THE HIGH CONTRACTING PARTIES SHALL SECURE TO

#5
ANONYMOUS

My name is [redacted]

I'm [redacted] year old

I came from [redacted]

Please
introduce yourself.

Q. 자기소개 부탁드립니다.

A. 제 이름은 -입니다. 전 -살이고 -에서 왔어요.

How long did it take for you to be granted 'indefinite leave to remain'?

I came here in 1991 so it is 18 years. I didn't know what ILR was because I came here to earn money to get job when I heard about ILR it was free to apply to UK abode so I didn't think it seriously. but it was raised to £750 when I decided to ~~apply~~ apply for ILR in 2008. I must have saved more money to do. my solisitor said the fee was £1820 when I was ready in 2009 and waited for one and half year until it was in my hand. This is why it took more than 14 years

Q. 14년 체류 규정을 받기까지 얼마나 걸렸나요?

A. 1991년 여기 왔으니 18년이 걸렸습니다. 돈을 벌고 일자리를 얻기 위해 왔기 때문에 ILR이 뭔지도 몰랐습니다. ILR에 대해 들었을 때, 신청하는 것이 무료였기 때문에 심각하게 생각하지 않았습니다. 하지만 2008년에 ILR 신청을 결심했을 때 수수료가 £750로 인상됐어요. 더 많은 돈을 저축해야만 했습니다. 2009년에 준비가 됐을 때 변호사가 수수료는 £1820라고 말했고, 제 손에 들어오기까지 1년 반이나 기다려야 했습니다. 그래서 14년 이상이 걸렸습니다.

I came here in 1991 so it is 18 years. I didn't know what ILR was because I came here to earn money to get job when I heard about ILR it was fee to apply to UK Border so I didn't think it seriously, but it was raised to £750 when I decided to apply for ILR in 2008. I must have saved more money to do. my solicitor said the fee was £820 when I was ready in 2009 and waited for one and half year until it was in my hand. That is why it took more than 14 years.

Have you been to
your country since you left?

No. I wasn't able to leave here to
anywhere because I had to prove how
long I was here and there musn't be a gap
I had to keep that. Also if I'd left here
how I could've come back here again?
there was no ~~[illegible]~~ solutions

Q. 고국을 떠나기로 한 이후로 다녀온 적이 있나요?

A. 아니요, 저는 여기를 떠나 어디로도 갈 수 없었어요. 왜냐하면 제가 여기에서 얼마나 오래 지냈는지 증명해야 했고, 체류 기간이 끊기면 안 됐거든요. 또, 여기를 떠났다면 어떻게 다시 돌아올 수 있겠어요? 해결책이 없었죠.

Have you been to your country since you left?

No. I wasn't able to leave here to anywhere because I had to prove how long I was here and there musn't be a gap. I had to keep that also if I'd left here how I could've come back here again? There was no ~~[illegible]~~ solutions.

Q. 고국을 떠나온 이후로 다녀온 적이 있나요?

A. 아니요, 저는 여기를 떠나 어디로도 갈 수 없었어요. 왜냐하면 제가 여기에 얼마나 오래 지냈는지 증명해야 했고 그 기간에 공백이 있으면 안 됐거든요. 또, 여기를 떠난다면 어떻게 다시 돌아올 수 있었겠어요? 해결책이 없었죠.

What made you decide to leave your own country?

I haven't told the reason except my family my
mother was raped when i was child and it
is very common in my county i didn't want to happen
the accident to my babies I decided to go the
UK to give a better and safer world to my
two daulters when my wife and I got the
twins.

Q. 고국을 떠나기로 한 이유는 무엇인가요?

A. 가족 외에는 이유를 말한 적이 없습니다. 제가 어렸을 때, 제 어머니가 성폭행을 당했습니다. 그리고 그런 범죄는 제 나라에서 매우 흔한 일입니다. 저는 제 아이들에게 그런 사고가 일어나길 원치 않았습니다. 제 아내가 쌍둥이를 가졌을 때, 두 딸에게 더 안전한 세상을 주고 싶어 영국행을 결정했습니다.

What made you decide to leave your own country?

I haven't told the reason except my family my mother was raped when I was child. and it is very common in my contry I didn't want to happen the accident to my babies. I decided to go the UK to give a better and safer world to my two daughters when my wife and I got the twins.

Q. 모국을 떠나기로 한 이유는 무엇인가요?

A. 가족 이외에는 이유를 말한 적이 없습니다. 제가 어렸을 때, 제 어머니가 성폭행을 당했습니다. 그리고 그런 일이 제 나라에서 매우 흔히 일어납니다. 저는 제 아이들에게 그런 사고가 일어나길 원치 않았습니다. 제 아내가 쌍둥이를 가졌을 때, 두 딸에게 더 안전한 세상을 주고 싶어 영국행을 결정했습니다.

Did you think you would have a better life in the UK when you left?

yes. absolutely If I didn't think
so. I wouldn't have left my family
for 18 years. the UK was regarded
much more advanced country than
my country. I thought there was
no problem if got a stable job
the present, I think there's no
problem if I got my own
house

Q. 고국을 떠날 때 영국에서 더 나은 삶을 살 수 있을 거라고 생각했나요?

A. 네, 확실히 그렇습니다. 그렇게 생각하지 않았다면, 가족을 18년 동안 떠나 있지 않았을 거예요. 영국은 제 나라보다 훨씬 더 발전된 나라로 여겨졌거든요. 제가 안정된 직장을 얻으면 문제가 없을 거라고 생각했어요. 제가 집을 구하면 문제가 없을 거라고요.

Did you think you would have
a better life in the UK when you left?

Yes, absolutely. If I didn't think so, I wouldn't have left my family for 18 years. The UK was regarded much more advanced country than my country. I thought there was no problem if I got a stable job. At the present, I think there's no problem if I got my own house.

Q. 고국을 떠날 때 영국에서 더 나은 삶을 살 수 있을 거라고 생각했나요?

A. 네, 확실히 그랬습니다. 그렇게 생각하지 않았다면, 가족을 18년 동안 떠나 있지 않았을 거예요. 영국은 제 나라보다 훨씬 더 발전된 나라로 여겨졌거든요. 제가 안정된 직장을 얻으면 문제가 없을 거라고 생각했어요. 지금은 제가 집을 구하면 문제가 없을 거라고요.

What was the most memorable experience during your time living in the UK illegally?

I hadn't eaten such the diliclous and rich food, pizza it is my favorit food still [illegible]

[illegible]

So I worked At Pizza shop and ate everyday for four mothes I really wanted to send it to my family and enjoy the taste together. One day, the master of the shop who was racist he beat me up everyday suspected me in my situation so I quit to shop and left another city

Q. 영국에서 불법으로 생활하는 동안 가장 기억에 남는 경험은 무엇인가요?

A. 저는 그렇게 맛있고 풍부한 빵, 피자를 먹어 본 적이 없습니다. 지금도 제가 제일 좋아하는 음식입니다. 그래서 피자 가게에서 일하며 4개월 동안 매일 피자를 먹었습니다. 정말, 가족에게 보내서 함께 맛보고 싶었습니다. 어느 날, 가게 주인이 제 체류 상황을 의심하면서 매일 저를 때렸기 때문에 가게를 그만두고 다른 도시로 떠났습니다.

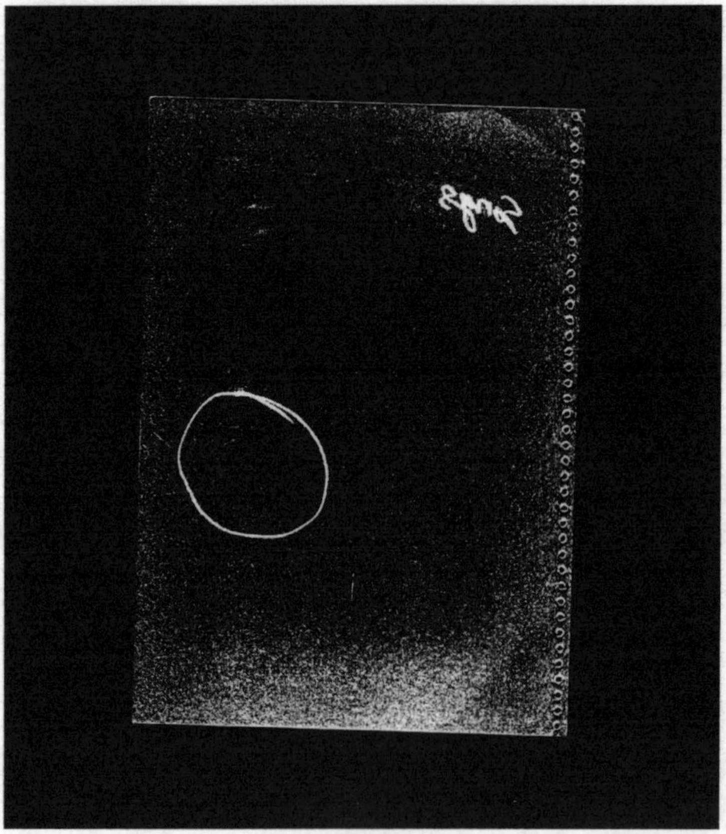

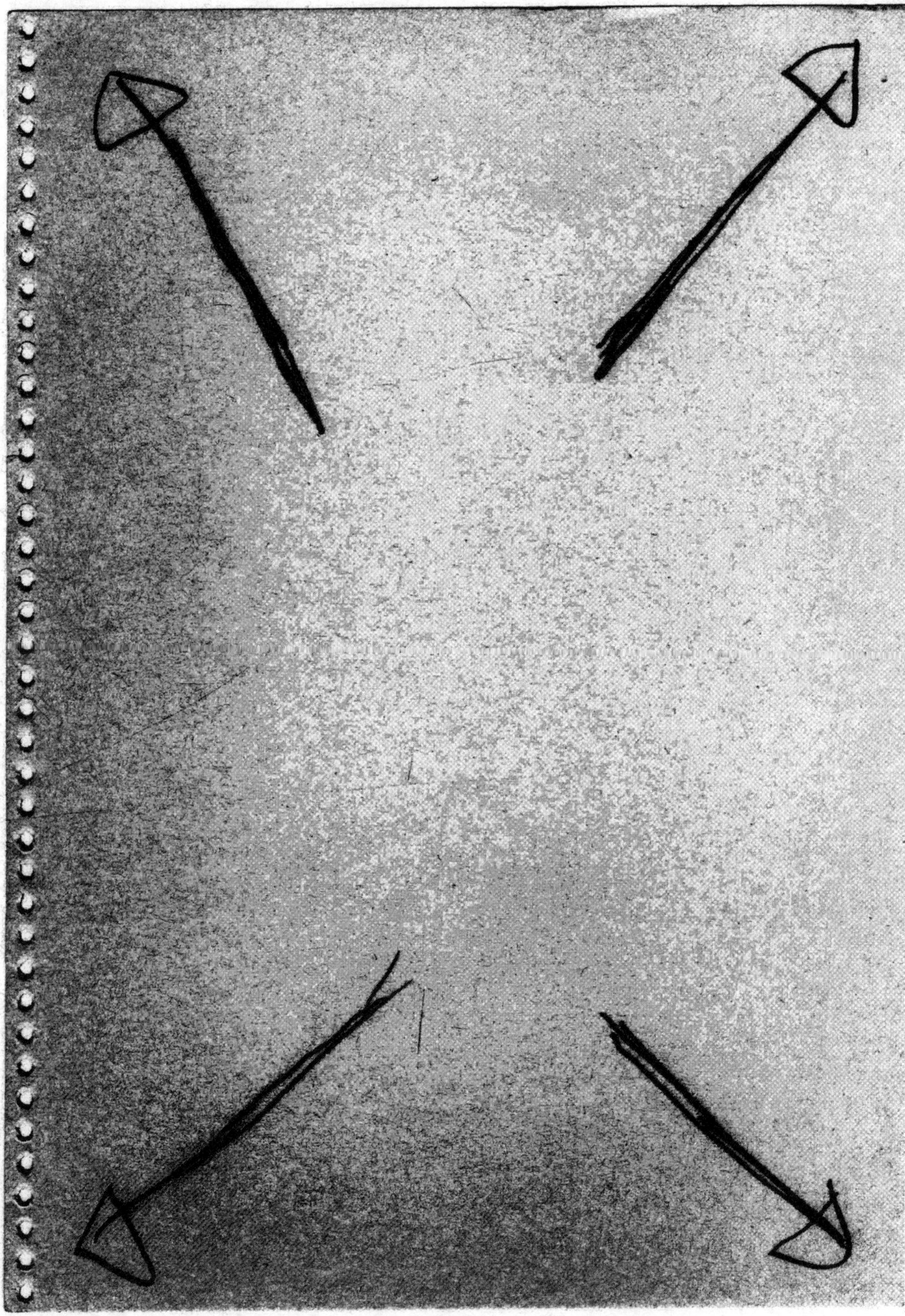

What are the most significant differences between being legal and illegal?

It is very obvious. people who I love are always with me I am not alone.

Q. 합법 체류와 불법 체류 사이의 가장 큰 차이점은 무엇인가요?

A. 매우 분명해요. 내가 사랑하는 사람들은 항상 저랑 같이 있어요. 저는 혼자가 아닙니다.

What is your impression of the UK?

I was shocked by rich foods and people didn't finish all their meal. It never happens in my country

Q. 영국에 대한 인상은 어땠나요?

A. 풍부한 음식에 놀랐고 사람들이 식사를 다 먹지 않는 것을 보고 충격을 받았습니다.
우리나라에서는 절대 일어나지 않는 일입니다.

What are the most significant differences between being legal and illegal?

It is very obvious. people who I love are always with me. I am not alone.

Q. 합법 체류와 불법 체류 사이의 가장 큰 차이점은 무엇인가요?

A. 매우 분명해요. 내가 사랑하는 사람들은 항상 저랑 같이 있어요. 저는 혼자가 아닙니다.

What is your impression of the UK?

I was shocked by rich foods and people didn't finish all their meal. It never happens in my country.

Q. 영국에 대한 인상은 어땠나요?

A. 풍부한 음식에 놀랐고 사람들이 식사를 다 먹지 않는 것을 보고 충격을 받았습니다. 우리나라에서는 절대 일어나지 않는 일입니다.

If you know someone, especially refugees or asylum seekers, who is considering using the '14-year rule' or contemplating living illegally in the UK, would you offer them any advice or recommendations?

may be not they should know
there's no gurantee they will bee
better. I can't recommend it. I'd better
say [illegible]

Q. 만약 당신이 아는 난민이나 망명 신청자가 '14년 규정'을 염두에 두거나 영국에서 불법 체류를 고려하고 있다면, 그들에게 어떤 조언이나 추천을 하겠습니까?

A. 아마도 삶이 더 나아질 것이라는 보장이 없다는 것을 알았으면 합니다. 추천할 순 없어요. 대신 -라고 말하고 싶습니다.

Why did you select the UK rather than another country?

I heard the UK government has more
open mind towards a refugee, but it used to
be, Not now.

Q. 왜 다른 나라 말고 영국을 선택했나요?

A. 영국 정부가 난민에게 더 개방적인 마음을 가지고 있다고 들었습니다. 하지만 그것은 과거의 일이고, 지금은 그렇지 않습니다.

If you know someone, especially refugees or asylum seekers, who is considering using the '10-year rule' or contemplating living illegally in the UK, would you offer them any advice or recommendations?

may be not they should know
there's no gurantee they can't bee
better. I can't recommend it. I'd better
say [illegible]

Q. [illegible]
[illegible]
A. [illegible]

Why did you select the UK rather than another country?

I heard the UK government has make
open mind towards a refugee, but it used to
be, Not now.

Q. [illegible]
A. [illegible]

자신의 가족을 직접 그린 인터뷰 대상자 #5 *Drawn his family by himself, #5 Anonymous*

If you were able to go back to the time when you made the decision to come here illegally, would you make the same choice?

Yes I would. I didn't overcome it for myself but for my family.
"My daughters" I wouldn't've accomplished it if it had been for only myself. I'd always do the same, even if I returned thousands of times to the past.

Q. 당신이 이곳에 불법 체류를 결정했던 시점으로 돌아갈 수 있다면, 같은 선택을 하겠습니까?

A. 네, 그렇게 할 겁니다. 제 자신을 위해서가 아니라 제 가족을 위해서요. 제 딸들 때문이죠. 저만을 위한 것이었다면 성취감을 느끼지 못했을 겁니다. 과거로 수천 번을 돌아간다 해도 항상 같은 선택을 할 거예요.

If you were able to go back to the time
when you made the decision to come here
illegally, would you make the same choice?

Yes I would. I didn't overcome it for myself but for my family.
"My daughters" I wouldn't've accomplished it if it had been for only myself I'd always do the same. even if I returned thousands of times to the past.

Q. 당신이 미국에 불법 체류를 결정했던 시점으로 돌아갈 수 있다면, 같은 선택을 하겠습니까?

A. 네, 그렇게 할 겁니다. 제 자신을 위해서가 아니라 제 가족을 위해서요. 제 딸들 때문이죠. 저만을 위한 것이었다면 성취감을 느끼지 못했을 겁니다. 과거로 수천 번을 돌아간다 해도 항상 같은 선택을 할 거예요.

Do you recall what your initial action was as soon as you were granted 'ILR'?

I did call my wife and we cried together for very long time

Q. <u>'ILR'을 부여받은 직후에 당신이 한 첫 번째 경험이 무엇인지 기억하나요?</u>

A. 제 아내와 함께 모든 것을 했고, 우리는 매우 오랜 시간 동안 함께 울었습니다.

Do you have something that you always keep with you?

I have my family pickture. It makes me much happier than the ILR

Q. 항상 가지고 다니는 물건이 있나요?

A. 제 가족사진이 있습니다. 이것은 ILR보다 저를 훨씬 더 행복하게 만듭니다.

**Are you happy with
how things are for you right now?**

yes I've lived with my family since
2010 my daughters study at a British
school. I've got a stable job everything
It is a night job. I'm very very happy

Q. 지금 당신의 현재 삶에 만족하고 있나요?

A. 네, 2010년부터 가족과 함께 살고 있고, 제 딸들은 영국 학교에서 공부합니다.
비록 야간 직업이지만 안정적인 일자리를 가지고 있습니다. 저는 매우 매우 행복해요.

Are you happy with how things are for you right now?

Yes I've lived with my family since 2010. my daughters study at a British school. I've got a stable job even though it is a night job. I'm very very happy.

Q. 지금 당신의 삶에 만족하고 있나요?

A. 네, 2010년부터 가족과 함께 살고 있고, 딸들은 영국 학교에서 공부합니다.
비록 야간 일이지만 안정적인 일자리를 가지고 있습니다. 저는 매우 매우 행복해요.

UK Border 

Opportunities

Bingo

1991 UK

97

2008 USA — 2009

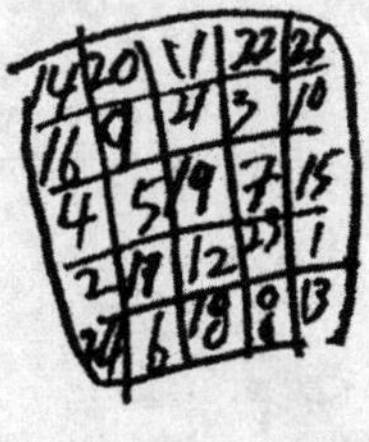

9

SIIY

NOTHING IN THIS DECLARATION MAY BE INTERPRETED AS IMPLYING FOR ANY ACT AIMED AT THE DESTRUCTION OF ANY OF THE RIGHTS AND FREEDOMS SET FORTH HEREIN.

이 선언의 어떠한 내용도 여기 명시된 권리와 자유를 파괴하려는
어떠한 행위를 할 수 있는 권리로 해석돼서는 안 된다. — 세계인권선언 제30조

Article 30 — The Universal Declaration Of Human Rights

MAY
AS IMPLYING FOR
ANY ACT AIMED AT
THE

SET

FORTH HEREIN

#6
ANONYMOUS

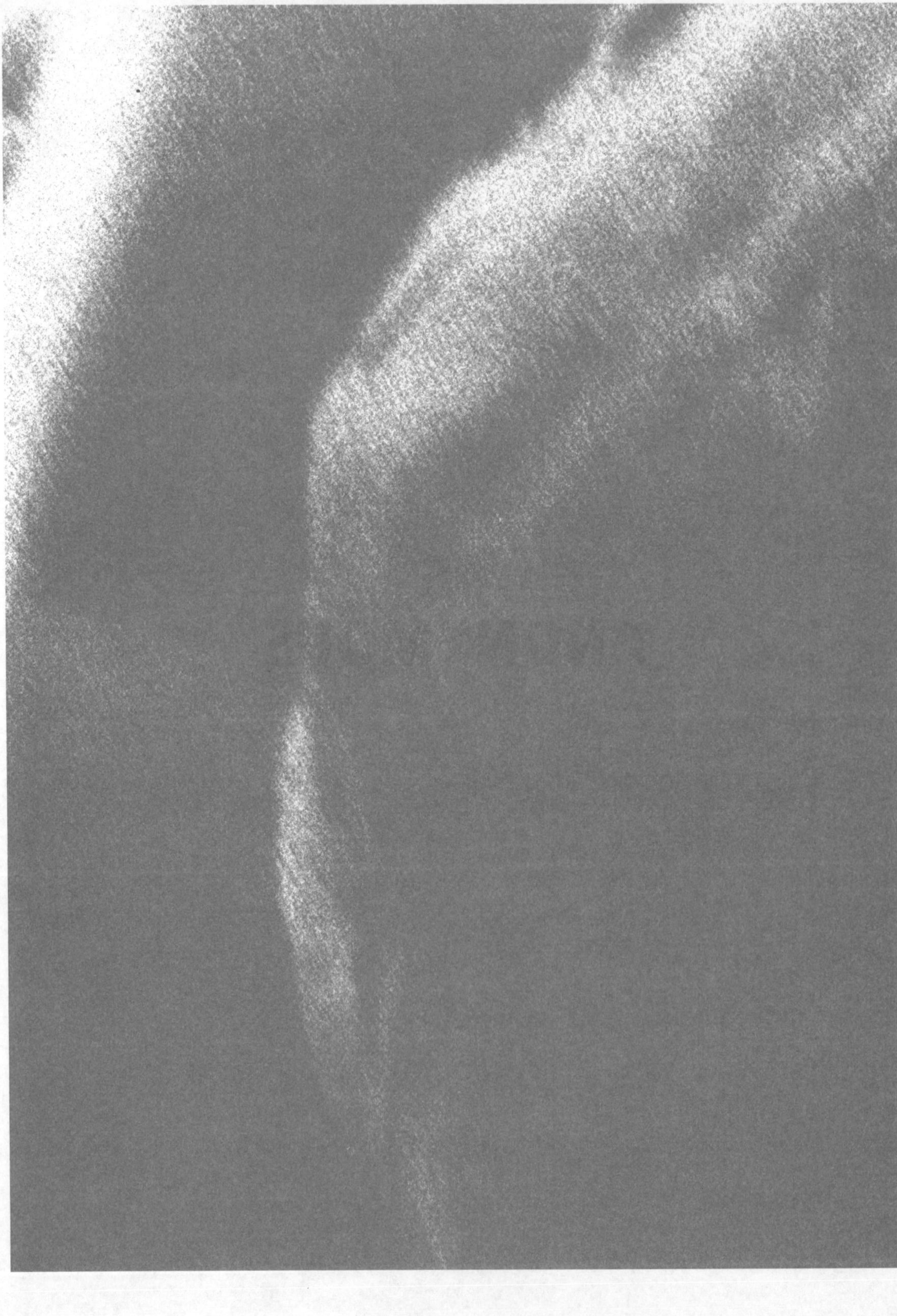

Please introduce yourself.

Q. 자기소개 부탁드립니다

I came from Pokhara-1, Kaski, Nepal.
My name is Ram ~~Bhadur~~ Bahadur Gurung.
I'm 58 yrs old married man.

A. 저는 네팔, 코스키 포카라에서 왔어요. 제 이름은 람 바하두르 구링입니다. 58살 기혼 남자입니다.

Please
introduce yourself.

Q. 자기소개 부탁드립니다.

How long did it take for you to be granted 'indefinite leave to remain'?

Q. 14년 체류 규정을 받기까지 얼마나 걸렸나요?

16 yrs. a came here in the year 1995 on May as a student

A. 16년이 걸렸어요. 1995년 5월, 학생으로 여기에 왔습니다.

What made you decide to leave your own country?

Q. 고국을 떠나기로 한 이유는 무엇인가요?

Because of Unemployment & provesty.
The first & foremost reason was UK is
prosperious country & it has lots of job opportunities.

A. 실업과 빈곤 때문입니다. 가장 큰 이유는 영국이 번영하는 나라이고 많은 일자리 기회가 있다는 것이었습니다.

Why did you select the UK rather than another country?

Q. 왜 다른 나라 말고 영국을 선택했나요?

at is good countay for
making a decent living.

A. 좋은 생활을 할 수 있는, 좋은 나라입니다.

How long did it take for you to be granted 'indefinite leave to remain'?

Q. 14년 체류 규정을 받기까지 얼마나 걸렸나요?

16 yrs to complete in the year 1995 on May as a student

A. 16년이 걸렸어요. 1995년 5월, 학생으로 여기에 왔습니다

What made you decide to leave your own country?

Q. 고국을 떠나기로 한 이유는 무엇인가요?

Because of [illegible]

[illegible]

A. [illegible]

Why did you select the UK rather than another country?

Q. 왜 다른 나라 말고 영국을 선택했나요?

It is good country for making a decent living

A. 좋은 생활을 할 수 있는 좋은 나라입니다

What is your impression of the UK?

Q. 영국에 대한 인상은 어땠나요?

When I first came here, I was surprised with the easy-going personalities & care-free attitude of natives.

A. 처음 여기에 왔을 때, 영국인들의 여유로운 성격과 걱정 없는 태도에 놀랐습니다.

Have you been to your country since you left?

Q. 고국을 떠나기로 한 이후로 다시 다녀온 적이 있나요?

Yeah, I had been to my country
last year after 17 yrs.
I was so happy to see my family
who came to greet
me at the airport. My happiness
had no boundaries then.

A. 네, 작년에 17년 만에 고향을 다녀왔어요. 공항에서 나를 맞이하러 온 가족들을 보고 너무 행복했어요.

What is your impression of the UK?

Q. 영국에 대한 인상은 어땠나요?

Have you been to your country since you left?

Q. 고국을 떠나기로 한 이후로 다시 다녀온 적이 있나요?

What was the most memorable experience during your time living in the UK illegally?

Q. 영국에서 불법으로 생활하는 동안 가장 기억에 남는 경험은 무엇이었나요?

My early day in this country when I had no jobs & money to pay rent. I ~~sleep on sofa~~ slept on sofa of living room in my friend's house.

A. 이 나라에서의 첫날, 일자리도 없고 임대료를 낼 돈도 없어 친구 집 소파에서 잠을 잤던 날입니다.

If you were able to go back to the time when you made the decision to come here illegally, would you make the same choice?

Q. 당신이 이곳에 불법 체류를 결정했던 시점으로 돌아갈 수 있다면, 같은 선택을 하겠습니까?

Yeah, I had no choice to come here. I had no job & decent life back in my country.

A. 네, 여기에 올 수밖에 없었습니다. 내 나라에는 일자리도 없고 제대로 된 삶도 없었습니다.

What was the most memorable experience during your time living in the UK illegally?

Q. 영국에서 불법으로 생활하는 동안 가장 기억에 남는 경험은 무엇이었나요?

If you were able to go back to the time when you made the decision to come here illegally, would you make the same choice?

Q. 당신이 이곳에 불법 체류를 결정했던 시점으로 돌아갈 수 있다면, 같은 선택을 하겠습니까?

Yeah, I had no choice to come here. I had no job & decent life back in my country.

What are the most significant differences between being legal and illegal?

Q. 합법체류와 불법 체류 사이의 가장 큰 차이점은 무엇인가요?

There is huge difference.
If any, I would say/point
about permit · work

A. 매우 큰 차이가 있습니다. 정확히는, 고용 허가라고 말할 수 있어요.

Do you recall what your initial action was as soon as you were granted 'ILR'?

Q. 'ILR'을 부여받은 직후에 당신이 한 첫 번째 경험이 무엇인지 기억하나요?

I was really happy.
Unexpectedly,
tears were rolling down to my cheeks.

A. 정말 행복했습니다. 생각지도 못한 일이라, 눈물이 줄줄 흘렀어요.

What are the most significant differences between being legal and illegal?

Q. 합법 체류와 불법 체류 사이의 가장 큰 차이점은 무엇인가요?

Do you recall what your initial action was as soon as you were granted 'ILR'?

Q. 'ILR'을 부여받은 직후에 당신이 한 첫 번째 행동이 무엇인지 기억하나요?

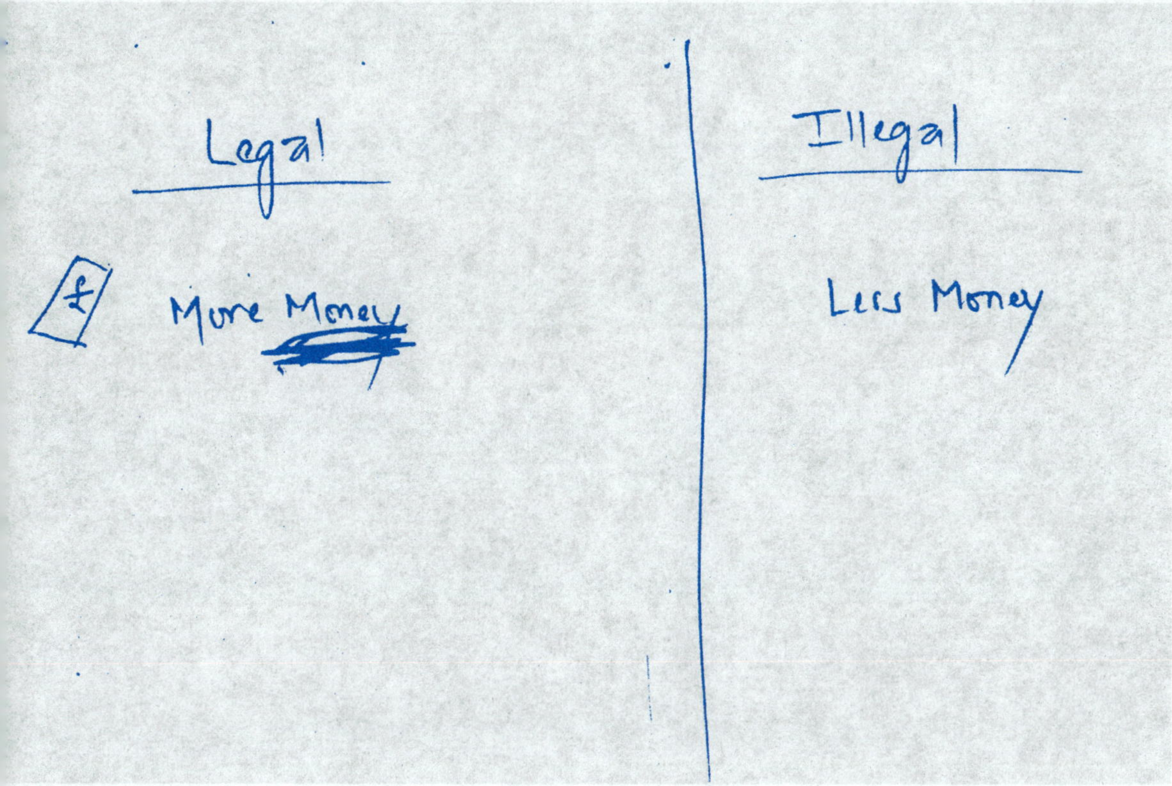
Legal
Illegal
£
More Money
Less Money

Have you confessed to or talked to anyone about your illegal situation?

Q. 불법 체류에 대해 고백하거나 누군가와 이야기한 적이 있나요?

Yeah, to many friends.
They were illegal like me.

A. 네, 많은 친구들과요. 그들도 저처럼 불법 상태였습니다.

If you know someone, especially refugees or asylum seekers, who is considering using the '14-year rule' or contemplating living illegally in the UK, would you offer them any advice or recommendations?

Q. 만약 당신이 아는 난민이나 망명 신청자가 '14년 규정'을 염두에 두거나 영국에서 불법 체류를 고려하고 있다면, 그들에게 어떤 조언이나 추천을 하겠습니까?

I would advice them to return back to their country. "Everyone deserve same respect & treatment being born as a fellow human but this "Illegal status" will always treat me as a low-life to human.

A. 자국으로 돌아가라고 조언하지는 않겠습니다. 모든 사람은 인간으로서 동등한 존중과 대우를 받을 자격이 있겠지만, 불법 체류 상태는 언제나 저를 낮은 수준의 인생으로 끌어내려요.

Have you confessed to or talked to anyone about your illegal situation?

Q. 불법 체류에 대해 고백하거나 누군가와 이야기한 적이 있나요?

If you know someone, especially refugees or asylum seekers, who is considering using the '14-year rule' or contemplating living illegally in the UK, would you offer them any advice or recommendations?

Q. 만약 당신이 아는 난민이나 망명 신청자가 '14년 규정'을 염두에 두거나 영국에서 불법 체류를 고려하고 있다면, 그들에게 어떤 조언이나 추천을 하겠습니까?

Did you think you would have a better life in the UK when you left?

Q. 당신은 고국을 떠날때 영국에서 더 나은 삶을 할 수 있을 거라고 생각했나요?

Yeah, but dream is dream
& reality is reality.

A. 네, 하지만 꿈은 꿈이고 현실은 현실입니다.

Do you have something that you always keep with you?

Q. 항상 가지고 다니는 물건이 있나요?

My daught's picture.
She was 2 ~~year~~ years old.

A. 제 딸의 사진입니다. 2살 때네요.

Are you happy with how things are for you right now?

Q. 지금 현재 삶에 만족하고 있나요?

Yeah.

A. 네.

Did you think you would have
a better life in the UK when you left?

Q. 당신은 고국을 떠날 때 영국에서
더 나은 삶을 살 수 있을 거라고
생각했나요?

Do you have something that
you always keep with you?

Q. 항상 가지고 다니는
물건이 있나요?

Are you happy with
how things are for you right now?

Q. 지금 현재 삶에
만족하고 있나요?

EVERYONE HAS THE RIGHT TO RESPECT FOR HIS PRIVATE AND FAMILY LIFE, HIS HOME AND HIS CORRES-PONDENCE.

모든 사람은 자신의 사생활과 가정생활, 주거 및 통신을 존중받을 권리가 있다. — 유럽인권협약 제8조

Article 8 — European Convention on Human Rights

EVERYONE
HAS

FOR

HIS

HIS AND
HIS CORRES-
PONDENCE

#7
ANONYMOUS

일곱번째 인터뷰이는 필적을 남기고 싶어 하지 않아, 영상 녹화로 이야기를 담았다.

#7 Anonymous preferred not to leave any handwriting, so his story was captured instead through a recorded video interview.

그러니까… 당신이 하려는 건 이런 이야기를 모아서 책에 담으려고 하는 거네요. 여러 사람들을 모아서 말이죠. 자, 어떤 질문을 할 건가요?

1992년에 여기 왔어요. 원래 학생은 주 20시간 일할 수 있지만, 실제로는 아무도 확인하지 않았죠. 계속 일을 했지만 아무도 제 기록에 대해 묻지 않았어요. 그래서 1998년에 지금 있는 이 회사에 갔을 때, 그들은 서류를 요구하지 않았고, 그냥 합류해서 계속 그곳에 있었어요. 정말 열심히 일했습니다. 공부하는 것보다 일하는 시간이 더 많았죠.

1992년에 여기에 와서 대학에서 회계 및 경영 정보 시스템을 공부했어요. 학위는 3년 걸려 1995년에 마쳤죠. 일자리를 찾아보았는데, 공인회계사가 되고 싶어서 계속 지원했지만, 거절 통지를 400통이나 받았어요. 그 후 석사 과정을 결심했습니다. 1995년부터 1996년까지 석사 과정을 전일제로 수학하고 1997년에 졸업했습니다. 졸업 후에 계속 일했는데, Tesco에서 했어요. 거기서 할 수 있는 거의 모든 일을 했어요. 그때 25살이었습니다.

So what you're trying to do is pick up this and show it in a book you're taking everyone so what questions you want to ask me.

In 92. Basically you could work as a student 20 hours, but no one checked. I kept working and no one asked me my papers. So in 98, when I went to this company, where I am, they weren't asking for papers. So, I just join and I stayed with them. I work hard. I was working more hours than I was studying.

What I did was I came here in 1992. I did a BSc in accounting and management information system at the University —. So that took 3 years, it took me to 1995. I looked for some jobs I had 400 letters of rejections. from chartered. I wanted to become a chartered accountant. I applied and applied and applied. I got 400 letter of rejections...

And then I decided to do a Masters. So, from 1995 to 1996, I did my Masters full time and graduated in 1997.

그러니까… 당신이 하려는 건 이런 이야기를 모아서 책에 담으려고 하는 거네요. 여러 사람들을 모아서 말이죠. 자, 어떤 질문을 할 건가요?

생계유지를 위해 무엇을 했고, 현재는 무엇을 하고 있나요?

1992년에 여기 왔어요. 원래 학생은 주 20시간 일할 수 있지만, 실제로는 아무도 확인하지 않았죠. 계속 일을 했지만 아무도 제 서류에 대해 묻지 않았어요. 그래서 1998년에 지금 있는 이 회사에 갔을 때, 그들은 서류를 요구하지 않았고, 그냥 합류해서 계속 그곳에 있었어요. 정말 열심히 일했습니다. 공부하는 것보다 일하는 시간이 더 많았죠.

1992년에 여기에 와서 대학에서 회계학, 경영 정보 시스템을 공부했어요. 학위는 3년 걸려 1995년에 마쳤죠. 일자리를 찾아보았는데, 공인회계사가 되고 싶어서 계속 지원했지만, 거절 통지만 400통이나 받았어요. 그 후 석사 과정을 결심했습니다. 1995년부터 1996년까지 석사 과정을 풀타임으로 수학하고 1997년에 졸업했습니다. 졸업 후에 계속 일했는데 Tesco에서 했어요. 거기서 할 수 있는 거의 모든 일을 했다가, 그때 정직원이 되었습니다.

So what you're trying to do is pick up this and show it in a book you're taking everyone so what questions you want to ask me.

What did and do you do for a living?

In 92. Basically you could work as a student 20 hours, but no one checked. I kept working and no one asked me my papers, so in 98, when I went to this company, where I am, they weren't asking for papers. So, I just join and I stayed with them. I work hard. I was working more hours than I was studying.

What I did was I came here in 1992. I do a BSc in accounting and management information system at the University — So that took 3 years, it took me to 1995. I looked for some jobs I had 400 letters of rejections, from chartered. I wanted to become a chartered accountant. I applied and applied and applied. I got 400 letter of rejections...

And then I decided to do a Masters. So, from 1995 to 1996, I did my Masters full time and graduated in 1997.

불법 체류를 시작한 동기는 무엇인가요?

일단, 저보다 열 살 어린 동생이 있어요. 저도, 동생도 공부를 계속하길 원해서 결정을 내렸죠. 그런데 1997년 7월에 아버지가 돌아가셔서 제가 박사 과정을 못하게 됐어요. 그래서 1997년부터 일을 시작했고, 2000년 3월까지 비자가 있었지만, 2000년 3월 31일이 됐을 때, 저는 영국을 떠나지 않고 계속 머물렀어요.

그냥 계속 일했죠. 일하고 또 일하고 계속 일했습니다. 상황을 합법화하기 위해 변호사를 만나러 갔고, 계속 일하다가 결국 변호사를 만났더니 14년 규정을 기다려야 한다고 말하더군요.

영국에 체류한 시간을 어떻게 증명했나요?

제가 모든 서류를 다 가지고 있었어요. 비자도 다 있었고, 집도 이미 산 상태였죠. 모든 게 다 있었기 때문에 그들이 저를 내치기 힘든 상황이었죠. 그리고 저는 많은 돈을 벌고 있었어요. 왜냐하면 저는 대학원 졸업자였으니까요. 제 석사 학위를 마쳤거든요. 그래도 3년이나 걸렸어요.

When I graduated in 1997. I worked for a bit and throughout all this time I was working, I was working in Tesco. So I worked for them, I sort of did everything. I need to do... I was 25 then...

What made you decide to be illegally?

Basically, my little brother, who's 10 years younger than me. He wanted, I wanted him to do his stud ies as well, so I took a decision. So when my father died in July 1997, I couldn't do my PhD, because my father passed away. So then I started working, so from 1997, I had Visa till 2000. March of 2000. 31st of March, 2000.

I got Visa. So I kept working and then when the 31st of March came, I didn't leave. I stay I stayed in the UK. when I stayed all that happened was, basically, I just kept on working. I worked and worked and worked. I went to see a solicitor to legalise the situation. when I sort of stayed and worked and worked and worked and worked. Finally, went to see a solicor and he said um he said I had to wait for the 14 year rule.

불법 체류를 시작한 동기는 무엇인가요?

일단 저보다 열 살 어린 동생이 있어요. 저는 동생도 공부를 계속하길 원했어요. 결정을 내렸죠. 그런데 1997년 7월에 아버지가 돌아가셔서 제가 박사 과정을 못하게 됐어요. 그래서 1997년부터 일을 시작했고, 2000년 3월까지 비자가 있었지만 2000년 3월 31일이 됐을 때, 저는 영국을 떠나지 않고 계속 머물렀어요.

그냥 계속 일했죠. 일하고 또 일하고 계속 일했습니다. 상황을 합법화하기 위해 변호사를 만나러 갔고, 계속 일하다가 결국 변호사를 만났더니 14년 규정을 기다려야 한다고 말하더군요.

영국에 머무른 시간을 어떻게 증명했나요?

제가 모든 서류를 다 가지고 있었어요. 편지도 다 있었고, 집도 하나 있었는데 모든 게 다 있었기 때문에 14년이 지난 뒤에 합법화할 수 있었죠. 그리고 저는 많은 돈을 벌고 있었어요. 테스코에 다닐 때 세금도 다 냈었어요. 계속해서 일을 했거든요. 그래서 증명이 됐어요.

When I graduated in 1997 I worked for a bit and throughout all this time I was working, I was working in Tesco. So I worked for them; I sort of did everything, I need to do it. I was 25 then...

What made you decide to be illegally?

Basically, my little brother, who's 10 years younger than me. He wanted, I wanted him to do his studies as well, so I took a decision. So when my father died in July 1997, I couldn't do my PhD, because my father passed away. So then I started working, so from 1997, I had visa till 2000. March of 2000. 31st of March 2000 I got Visa. So I kept working and then when the 31st of March came, I didn't leave. I stay I stayed in the UK, when I stayed all that happened was, basically, I just kept on working, I worked and worked and worked. I went to see a solicitor to legalise the situation, when I sort of stayed and worked and worked and worked and worked. Finally went to see a solicitor and he said um he said I had to wait for the 14 year rule...

여기에 'ILR'을 얻으려고 계획하고 왔습니까?

아니요, 공부하러 여기 왔어요. 그냥 공부하러 왔을 뿐이에요, 그러니까 저는 기본적으로 공부만 했죠.

지금은 어떤 일을 하시나요?

저는 한 회사의 대표예요. 우리나라에 그 자회사를 설립했고, 저는 거기서도 책임을 맡고 있어요.

왜 다른 나라 말고 영국을 선택했나요?

영국 교육이 제일 좋거든요. 그래서 공부하러 왔습니다.

14년 넘게 기다리고 받은 'ILR'을 받은 기분이었나요?

우선, 제가 변호사에게서 제 서류를 받았다는 편지를 받았을 때, 전화해서 "정말 제 서류 맞아요?"라고 물었어요. 믿기지가 않았거든요. 그랬더니 변호사가 "네, 맞습니다" 하더라고요.

How did you prove the time you stayed in the UK to Home Office?

I had all my documents. I had all my visas, I already had bought the house. I had everything. So it was very difficult for them to refuse to me. And I was earning a lot of money. So, for them it was difficult. Because, I was a graduate and a postgraduate. I was my Masters. So, but it took 3 years still.

Did you come here deliberately to get ILR?

No, I came here a to study. I just came here a to study and I just basically, I studied...

Whata do you do for living?

I'm managing director, at a company. And the company now, the company is opened a subsidiary in my country and I'm in charge ther as well.

"알겠어요, 월요일에 찾으러 갈게요"라고 했죠. 그리고 다시 전화해서 "내일 문 열어요?"라고 물었습니다. 변호사가 "네"라고 대답했고, 저는 바로 받으러 갔어요. 제 여권을 손에 쥐기 전까지는 믿을 수가 없었어요. 너무 오랫동안 기다리면, 믿음과 희망이 사라지잖아요. 맞아요, 3년은 정말 긴 시간이죠. 그런데 3년도 아니었어요. 신청하기 전 6년을 더 기다렸으니까. 총 9년이었고, 할 수 있는 건 아무것도 없었어요. 그저 기다리기만 했죠.

합법 체류와 불법 체류 사이의 가장 큰 차이점은 무엇인가요?

한 가지 말씀드리자면, 인간 본성이란 건 이런 거예요. 무언가 없으면 그것을 갖고 싶어 하죠. 한 번 갖게 되면 다음엔 또 다른 걸 원하게 되는 거죠. 그게 뭐 중요하겠어요? 제가 생각하기엔, 다른 나라에서 살면 어떨까 하는 생각도 들죠. 그게 인간 본성이에요. 가장 큰 차이는 이제 저는 거리를 걸을 때 걱정할 필요가 없어요. 사실 신경 쓸 필요도 없죠. 저는 꽤 행복해요. 자유롭게 다닐 수 있다는 것, 그게 큰 차이죠.

Why did you select the UK rather than another country?

Because, UK has the best education.
So, I came here to study.

How did you feel when you got ILR after over 14 years?

Basically, when I... when I got my letter from the solicitor to say, I got my paper I rang the solicitor and said "Are you sure, you got my paper?" Because, I couldn't believe. And then he said "Yeah, I'm sure" I said "Okay, I'll come and get it". It was a Friday. I said "I'd come and get it on Monday" and then I rank them again. and I said "Are you open tomorrow:", he said "Yeah". So I went to get it, bcause I was scared, untill my passport was in my hands. I wouldn't believe. Because, when you wait so long you, don't you stop believing, stop hoping. So yeah, 3 years is a long time to wait. That was not 3 years. And before, I waited 6 years to apply. So it was like so you wait 9 years, you couldn't do anything.

Just wait.

합법 체류와 불법 체류 사이의 가장 큰 차이점은 무엇인가요?

Why did you select the UK rather than another country?

How did you feel when you got ILR after over 14 years?

아무에게도 알리지 않았어요. 당신이 이 사실을 알게 된 첫 번째 사람이에요.

영국이 예전 같지 않아요. 이제 우리나라가 얼마나 발전했는지 보니까, 제가 그냥 거기에 남았더라면 더 나았을 거 같아요.

그래요, 난 항상… 그랬을 거예요. 하지만 제가 말하고 싶은 건, 만약 지금 누군가가 "다시 하겠어?"라고 묻는다면, 저는 안 할 거예요. 하지만 젊었을 때를 돌이켜 보면, 그 경험이 저에게 인내심과 성격을 길러 주었고, 저는 여전히 행복해요. 슬프지 않아요.

I'll tell you one thing, yeah. The only difference, human nature is like this, when they don't have something, you want it. Once you got it, then you look for something else that, then you look for something else that you don't have. It doesn't matter. I can say is, I think to myself, Oh wouldn't be nice living other countries. That's human nature. The big difference is now, I can walk in the street, I don't have to worry. Basically, I don't have to care. I'm quite happy.

I'm free to come and go and that's a big difference.

I never let anyone know. You're the first person that really knows about it.

불법 체류에 대해 고백하거나
누군가와 이야기한 적이
있나요?

만약 당신이 아는 난민이나
망명 신청자가 '14년 규정'을
염두에 두거나 외국에서 불법
체류를 고려하고 있다면,
그들에게 어떤 조언이나
추천을 하겠습니까?

당신이 이곳에 불법 체류를
결정했던 시점으로 돌아갈 수
있다면, 같은 선택을 하겠습니까?

What are the most
significant differences
between being legal
and illegal?

Have you confessed to or
talked to anyone about
your illegal situation?

항상 가지고 다니는 물건이 있나요?

다 내 마음속에 있어요. 기본적으로 항상 최선을 바라야 해요. 최선을 바라지 않으면 살아가는 의미가 없죠.

ILR을 부여받은 직후에 당신이 한 첫 번째 경험이 무엇인지 기억나나요?

항공사에 전화해서 표를 예약했어요. 바로 받자마자 전화했고, 가격이 얼마든 상관없었어요. 그냥 갔어요. 그리고 그 이후로 18개월 동안 10번이나 갔어요. 자주 가니까 이제 골드 카드를 받았어요.

마지막으로, 왜 인터뷰를 하기로 결심했나요?

이야기를 풀어놓으면, 제가 그 상황에 있을 때가 늘 기억나요. 제가 그런 상황에 처해 있을 때 누군가 자기 이야기를 들려주길 바랐는데 그런 사람이 없었어요. 다른 사람을 생각하는 건 정말 중요하다고 생각해요. 그게 제가 이 인터뷰를 하고 싶은 이유예요. 제가 어떤 기분이었는지 알기 때문이죠. 인생에서 다른 사람들이 겪는 일을 이해하는 건 정말 중요해요.

그리고 그들에게 이야기를 들려주는 것도요.
정말 중요하죠.

If you know someone, especially refugees or asylum seekers, who is considering using the '14-year rule' or contemplating living illegally in the UK, would you offer them any advice or recommendations?

England is not qualities. What it is...used to. Now, having seen, how much my own country has developed. I think, I would have been better off had I stayed.

If you were able to go back to the time when you made the decision to come here illegally, would you make the same choice?

Yeah, I would always...

I would have done it. But what I'm saying is, if now, someone said "Would you do it again?, I wouldn't. But if when I look back to when I was younger, because what it gave me is patience, character and I'm still happy. I'm not sad

항상 가지고 다니는 물건이 있나요?

'ILR'을 부여받은 직후에 당신이 한 첫 번째 경험이 무엇인지 기억하나요?

마지막으로, 왜 인터뷰를 하기로 결정했나요?

If you know someone, especially refugees or asylum seekers, who is considering using the '14-year rule' or contemplating living illegally in the UK, would you offer them any advice or recommendations?

If you were able to go back to the time when you made the decision to come here illegally, would you make the same choice?

Do you have something that you always keep with you?

It's all here my mind. Basically, you've always got to hope for the best. If you don't hope for the best, there's no point living.

Do you recall what your initial action was as soon as you were granted 'ILR'?

I phoned airlines and I book my ticket. As soon as I got it, I phoned, it didn't matter how much it cost. I just went. And since then, I've gpne 10 times in 18 months. And because, I've gone so much and now, gold card.

Finally, why did you desided to have this interview?

Because, if you tell the story, I always remember... when I was in that situation, I wanted someone to tell me their story and there wasn't anyone. Yeah, I think it's very important to think of other people. That's what I want to do. Because, I know how I felt. I think it's very important in life to understand what other people go through.

And to tell them a story... You know, it's very important.

Do you have something that you always keep with you?

Do you recall what your initial action was as soon as you were granted 'ILR'?

Finally, why did you desided to have this interview?

THESE RIGHTS AND FREEDOMS MAY IN NO CASE BE EXERCISED CONTRARY TO THE PURPOSES AND PRINCIPLES OF THE UNITED NATIONS

이 권리와 자유는 어떤 경우에도 유엔의 목적과 원칙에 반하여 행사될 수 없다. — 세계인권선언 제29조 3항

Article 29 — The Universal Declaration Of Human Rights

THESE
MAY
IN
THE PURPOSES AND
PRINCIPLES OF

'14년 규정'의 기원

영주권 취득을 위한 '14년 규정'은 영국 이민법에 포함된 특별 조항으로서, 특정 조건하에서 불법 이민자가 합법적으로 영국 내에 거주할 수 있는 통로를 제공했다. '14년 규정'은 영국에서 14년 동안 연속적으로 거주한 불법 이민자들에게 법적 지위와 관계없이 영구 거주를 신청할 수 있도록 허용했다. 이는 복잡한 인권 문제와 함께 실용적인 이민 문제를 해결하려는 이민 정책 체계의 중요한 측면을 반영한다.

'14년 규정'이 제정된 역사적 배경으로 주요 사건과 입법적 변화를 빼놓을 수 없다. 2000년, 도버항을 통해 밀입국한 58명의 중국 이민자가 컨테이너 안에서 숨진 채 발견된 사건이 발생했다.[1] 이를 포함한 비극적 사건들의 영향으로 영국 이민 시스템에 심각한 결함이 있다는 사실이 수면 위로 드러나며 망명 및 이민 정책을 재평가할 필요성이 제기됐다. 그 결과로 「국적, 이민 및 망명법」(The Nationality, Immigration and Asylum Act, NIA)이 2002년에 제정, 2003년 4월에 시행되면서 영국 이민법에 상당한 개혁이 이루어졌다.

2002년 출간된 『안전한 국경, 안전한 피난처』(Secure Borders, Safe Haven)라는 제목의 백서에서 '관리된 이주'(managed migration)라는 개념이 제안됐다. 이 개념은

1. 발견된 58구의 시신과 서류를 파기한 중국 국적자들을 다시 받아들이기를 거부한 베이징 정부의 결정을 말한다. 이 거부로 인해 이민 당국은 수백 명의 실패한 중국 망명 신청자를 추방하려는 시도가 좌절됐다.

The Root

The 14-year rule for Indefinite Leave to Remain (ILR) was a distinctive provision in the UK's immigration law, offering a pathway for illegal immigrants to legally reside in the country under certain conditions. This rule allowed individuals who had lived continuously in the UK for 14 years, regardless of their legal status, to apply for permanent residency, reflecting a significant aspect of the immigration framework that sought to address complex human rights issues as well as pragmatic immigration concerns.

The historical backdrop of the 14-year rule was marked by pivotal events and legislative changes. The Nationality, Immigration and Asylum Act (NIA) enacted in 2002 and implemented in April 2003 introduced substantial reforms to the immigration laws. These reforms were influenced by incidents such as the tragic death of 58 Chinese immigrants in 2000[1], who were found in a refrigerated lorry in Dover. This event

1. This refers to the discovery of 58 bodies and the refusal of the Beijing government to take back Chinese nationals who had destroyed their documents. This refusal blocked the immigration authorities' attempts to remove hundreds of failed Chinese asylum seekers.

14년 규정의 기원

영주권 취득을 위한 '14년 규정'은 영국 이민법에 포함된 특별 조항으로서, 특정 조건하에서 불법 이민자가 합법적으로 영국 내에 거주할 수 있는 통로를 제공했다. [redacted] 이는 복잡한 인권 문제와 함께 실용적인 이민 문제를 해결하려는 이민 정책 체계의 중요한 측면을 보여준다.

[redacted] 주요 사건과 입법적 변화를 특징으로 할 수 [redacted] 있다. [redacted] 이를 철폐하려는 사건들의 영향으로 영국 이민 시스템에 심각 [redacted] 한 결함이 있다는 사실이 수면 위로 드러나며 했다. 그 결과로 국적, 이민 및 망명법(The Nationality, Immigration and Asylum Act, NIA)이 2002년에 제정, 2003년 4월에 시행되면서 영국 이민법에 상당한 개혁이 이루어졌다.

2002년 출간된 '안전한 국경, 안전한 피난처(Secure Borders, Safe Haven)' 백서에서 '관리된 이주(managed migration)'라는 개념이 제안되고 이 개념은

The Root

The 14-year rule for Indefinite Leave to Remain (ILR) was a distinctive provision in the UK's immigration law, offering a pathway for illegal immigrants to legally reside in the country under certain conditions. [redacted] reflecting a significant aspect of the immigration framework that sought to address complex human rights issues as well as pragmatic immigration concerns.

[redacted] marked by pivotal events and legislative changes. The Nationality, Immigration and Asylum Act (NIA) enacted in 2002 and implemented in April 2003 introduced substantial reforms to the immigration laws. These reforms were [redacted] This event [redacted]

합법적인 이주 통로를 마련하는 동시에 경제 이민자들이 망명 체계를 악용하는 문제에 대한 방안과 저숙련 노동자의 입국을 규제하고 이민자들을 영국 노동 시장에 효과적으로 흡수시켜야 한다는 필요성에 대응하는 방안을 제시했다. 이러한 이민 정책은 인권 고려 사항과 깊이 얽혀 있다. 국제법의 초석이라고 할 수 있는 유럽인권협약(The European Convention on Human Rights, ECHR)[2]은 인권을 존중하고 보호하며 실현해야 할 국가의 의무를 강조하는 법적 틀을 마련했다. 국가 안보 문제에 대응하는 동시에 개인의 권리 보호를 위한 원칙을 반영하는 방향으로 발전했다는 점에서, 영국의 이민 규정이 ECHR의 영향을 받았음을 알 수 있다.

2. ECHR은 유럽 내 인권 보호의 핵심적인 역할을 하는 문서로, 이를 통해 유럽 시민들은 다양한 기본적 권리와 자유를 보호받을 수 있다. 또한 유럽 인권 재판소를 통해 실질적인 법적 구제를 받을 수 있는 기회를 제공한다.

'14년 규정'의 시행 및 점진적 폐지 과정을 살펴보면, 영국이 이민자의 권리와 공익을 균형 있게 조정하기 위해 노력했다는 사실을 확인할 수 있다. '14년 규정'은 장기 체류 이민자의 합법화를 촉진했으나, 이민 정책의 공정성과 의미에 대한 논쟁을 촉발하기도 했다. 「텔레그래프」(The Telegraph)의 보도에서 강조한 바와 같이, 언론과 공공 포럼에서의 토론은 안전한 국경 보호를 주장하는 세력과 인권 보호를 옹호하는 세력 간의 긴장을 고조시켰다.[3]

3. 텔레그래프는 영국 내 불법 이민자의 숫자가 증가하고 있으며, 이들이 14년 동안 체류한 후 합법적으로 정착할 수 있게 됨에 따라 이민 정책이 악용될 수 있다는 점을 지적했다. 이는 영국 정부가 이민 정책을 보다 엄격하게 관리할 필요성을 강조하는 배경이 됐다.

요약하자면, '14년 규정'의 변천 과정을 분석함으로써 영국의 이민 정책, 인권, 사회적 가치관이 어떻게 상호 작용했는지 알 수 있다. 이러한 분석은 국가가 국제법 및 인권 보호 의무를 준수하면서 이민자를 관리하고 이들을 사회에 통합하는 방법에 관한 폭넓은

---

highlighted severe deficiencies in the UK's immigration system and prompted a reevaluation of asylum and immigration policies.

The 2002 white paper titled 'Secure Borders, Safe Haven' proposed the concept of 'managed migration.' This initiative aimed to create legal avenues for migration and address the exploitation of the asylum system by economic migrants. It was a response to the growing need to regulate the entry of low-skilled workers and to better manage the integration of immigrants into the UK labor market.

These immigration policies were deeply intertwined with human rights considerations. The European Convention on Human Rights (ECHR), a cornerstone of international law, provided a legal framework that underscored the obligation of states to respect, protect, and fulfill human rights.[2] The ECHR's influence is evident in the way the UK's immigration rules evolved to incorporate principles that safeguard individual rights while addressing national security concerns.

2. The ECHR is a fundamental document for the protection of human rights in Europe, allowing European citizens to safeguard various basic rights and freedoms. Additionally, it provides the opportunity for substantial legal remedies through the European Court of Human Rights.

[illegible]

[redacted]

[illegible]

[redacted]

[illegible]

[redacted]

[illegible]

[illegible]

highlighted severe deficiencies in the UK's immigration system and

[redacted]

The 2002 white paper titled 'Secure Borders, Safe Haven' proposed the concept of 'managed migration.' This initiative aimed to create legal avenues for migration and address the exploitation of the asylum system by economic migrants. It was a response to the growing need to regulate the entry of low-skilled workers and to better manage the integration of immigrants into the UK labor market.

[redacted] The ECHR's influence is evident in the way the UK's immigration rules evolved to incorporate principles that safeguard individual rights while addressing national security concerns.

논의를 불러일으킨다. '히든 사이드 프로젝트'는 이민 정책의 복잡성을 조명하는 데에서 그치지 않고, 우리로 하여금 변화하는 사회적, 경제적, 정치적 압력에 대응하여 법적 틀이 어떻게 변화해 왔는지 더욱 깊이 이해하도록 돕는다.

The implementation and eventual phase-out of the 14-year rule illustrate the UK's efforts to balance public interest with the rights of immigrants. This rule not only facilitated the regularization of long-standing immigrants but also sparked debates about the fairness and implications of such policies. Discussions in the media and public forums, as highlighted by reports in The Telegraph, underscored the tensions between maintaining secure borders and upholding human rights.[3]

In summary, the evolution of the 14-year rule showcases the dynamic interplay between immigration policy, human rights, and societal values in the UK. It reflects a broader dialogue about how nations manage migration and integrate immigrants into their societies while adhering to international law and human rights obligations. This analysis not only sheds light on the complexities of immigration policies but also contributes to a deeper understanding of how legal frameworks develop in response to changing social, economic, and political pressures.

3. The Telegraph pointed out that the number of illegal immigrants in the UK is increasing, and that the 14-year rule, which allows them to settle legally after staying for 14 years, could be exploited. This highlights the need for the UK government to manage immigration policies more strictly.

노인들 불러일으킨다. '히든 사이드 프로젝트'는 이미 잠재력의 가치성을 조명하는 데에서 그치지 않고, [redacted]

[redacted] This rule not only facilitated the regularization of long-standing immigrants but also sparked debates about the fairness and implications of such policies. Discussions in the media and public forums, as highlighted by reports in The Telegraph, underscored the tensions between maintaining secure borders and upholding human rights.

In summary, the evolution of the 14-year rule showcases the dynamic interplay between immigration policy, human rights, and societal values in the UK. It reflects a broader dialogue about how nations manage migration and integrate immigrants into their societies while adhering to international law and human rights obligations. This analysis not only sheds light on the complexities of immigration policies but also [redacted]

14년이라는 기간은 누구에게도 짧지 않다. 불법 이민자에 관한 대중의 인식 및 ILR 관련 특정 규정에 관한 그들의 태도를 더욱 깊이 이해하고자 영국인을 대상으로 '14년 거주 영주권' 및 '20년 거주 영주권'에 관한 설문조사를 실시했다.

The period of 14 years is not short for anyone. To better understand and explain the public's perception of illegal immigrants and attitudes towards specific rules regarding ILR, a survey was conducted among the British regarding the 14-year and 20-year ILR.

영국으로 이주해 현재 불법으로 거주하는 이민자 수가 과거에 비해 증가 / 감소 / 비슷하다고 생각합니까?

6%	잘 모르겠다
81%	증가했다
13%	비슷하다
0%	감소했다

SOURCE:
20.02.2013 TO 19.04.2013
(n=181)

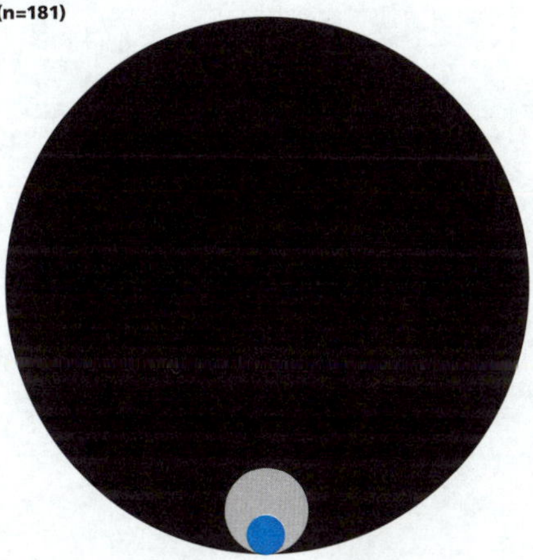

When considering the current population of illegal immigrants coming to and living in Britain, do you believe it has increased, reduced, or remained similar to that in the past?

6%	Don't know
81%	Increased
13%	Simlar
0%	Decreasd

영국 내 불법 이민자들이라고 하면, 어떤 이유로 이주한 사람들이 주로 떠오릅니까?

53%	망명
31%	취업
10%	공부
6%	잘 모르겠다

SOURCE:
14.01.2012 TO 13.02.2012

ALL RESPONDENTS
(n=169)

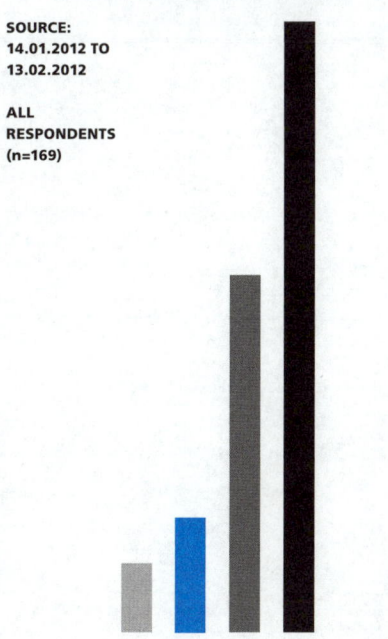

When considering illegal immigrants coming to and living in Britain, which of these groups do you typically think about?

53%	Asylum
31%	Work
10%	Study
6%	Don't know

영국 내 불법 이민자들을 부정적인 시각으로 바라봅니까?

84%	그렇다
11%	관심 없다
5%	아니다

SOURCE:
14.01.2012 TO
13.02.2012
(n=169)

When considering the population of illegal immigrants coming to and living in Britain, do you hold a negative stance toward them?

84%	Yes
11%	Do not care
5%	No

14년 이상 영국에 거주한 외국인에게 영주권을 부여하는 일종의 사면 제도인 '14년 규정' 또는 '20년 규정'에 관해 들어 본 적이 있습니까?

4%	들어 본 적 있다
96%	들어 본 적 없다

SOURCE:
14.01.2012 TO
13.02.2012
(n=169)

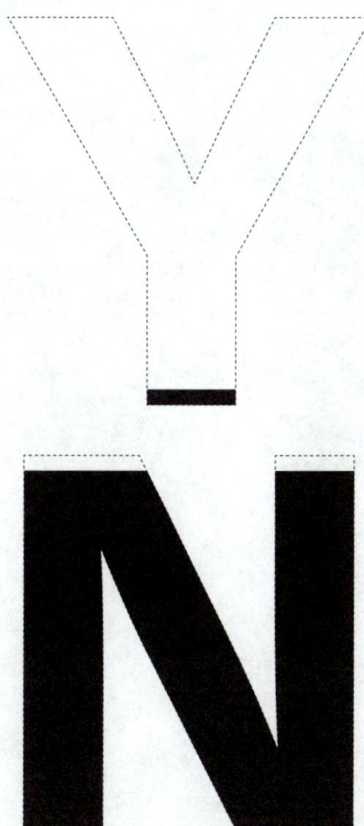

Have you heard about the 14-year rule or 20 years' residence, a form of amnesty that allows overstayers to legalise their stay in the UK after 14 years?

4%	Yes
96%	No

14년 동안 불법적으로 영국에 거주한 사람들이 영주 비자를 받을 자격이 있다고 생각합니까?

1%	그렇다
23%	잘 모르겠다
76%	아니다

SOURCE:
(top)
14.01.2012 TO
13.02.2012
(n=169)

(bottom)
20.02.2013 TO
19.4.2013
(n=181)

Do you believe they deserve to be granted a permanent visa after residing in the UK illegally for 14 years?

1%	Yes
23%	Do not know
76%	No

20년 동안 불법적으로 영국에 거주한 사람들이 영주 비자를 받을 자격이 있다고 생각합니까?

59%	아니다
27%	그렇다
14%	잘 모르겠다

Do you think they deserve to be granted a permanent visa after residing in the UK illegally for 20 years?

59%	No
27%	Yes
14%	Do not know

14년 규정과 20년 규정은 모든 사람이 박해를 피해 다른 나라에서 망명을 신청하고 누릴 수 있는 권리를 보장해야 한다는 인권 보호 조약에 따라 제정됐습니다. 이러한 규정이 불법 이민자들에게 합리적이라고 생각합니까?

53%	아니다
27%	그런 것 같다
11%	그렇다
9%	잘 모르겠다

SOURCE:
20.02.2013 TO
19.4.2013
(n=181)

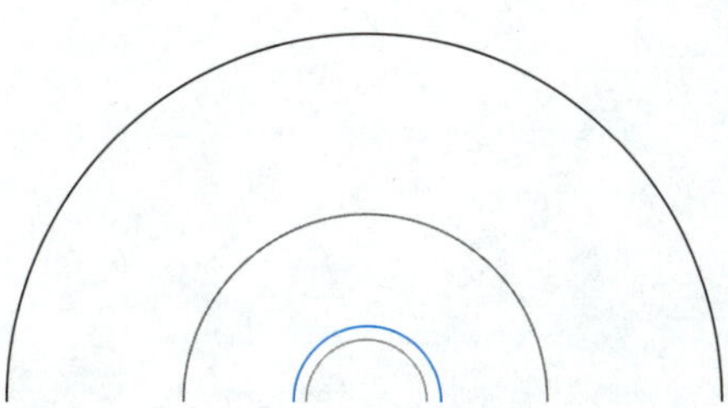

The 14-year rule and 20-year rule have been established under human rights, affirming everyone's right to seek and enjoy asylum from persecution in other countries. Do you find this provision reasonable for irregular migrants?

53%	No
27%	Somewhat
11%	Yes
9%	I don't know

불법 이민자 수를 줄이기 위한 정책을 지지합니까?

39%	(매우) 그렇다
21%	(대체로) 그렇다
18%	관심 없다
6%	(대체로) 그렇지 않다
6%	(매우) 그렇지 않다
10%	잘 모르겠다

SOURCE:
(top)
14.01.2012 TO 13.02.2012 (n=169)
(bottom)
20.02.2013 TO 19.4.2013 (n=181)

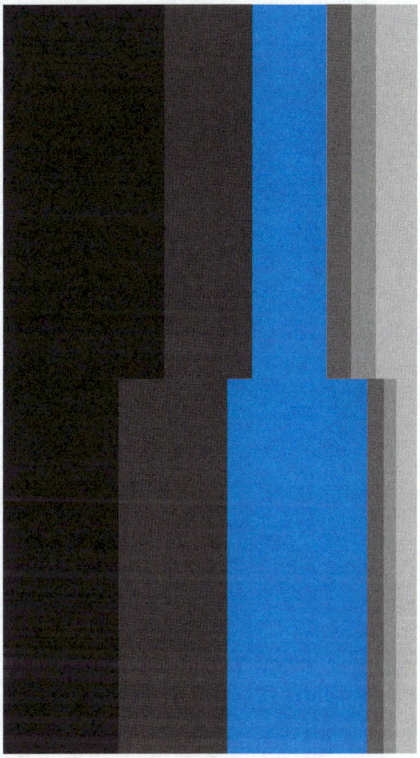

Do you support policies aimed at reducing the number of illegal immigrants?

39%	Yes (feel strongly)
21%	Yes (tend to feel)
18%	Don't mind
6%	No (tend to feel)
6%	NO (feel strongly)
10%	Don't know

다음 중 어느 집단에서 이민자 수를 줄이는 것이 더 바람직하다고 생각합니까?

28%	불법 체류자만 줄여야 한다
26%	불법 체류자 위주로 줄여야 한다
34%	동등하게 줄여야 한다
4%	합법 체류자 위주로 줄여야 한다
3%	합법 체류자만 줄여야 한다
5%	잘 모르겠다

Which of these groups would you prefer to see reduced immigration among?

28%	Only illegal
26%	Mostly illegal
34%	Equally
4%	Mostly legal
3%	Only legal
5%	Don't know

영국에 불법으로 거주하다가 영주권(Indefinite Leave to Remain, ILR)을 취득한 이민자들이 현재 상황에 만족한다고 생각합니까?

2%	만족하지 않을 것이다
17%	잘 모르겠다
81%	만족할 것이다

SOURCE:
14.01.2012 TO 13.02.2012 (n=169)

Do you believe individuals who attain Indefinite Leave to Remain (ILR) after residing in the UK illegally will be content with their current circumstances?

2%	No, they would not
17%	I do not know
81%	Yes, they would

References

ARTICLE 8: THE RIGHT TO RESPECT FOR PRIVATE AND FAMILY LIFE, HOME AND CORRESPONDENCE

BLINDER, SCOTT. "PUBLIC OPINION AND PUBLIC POLICY: COMPLEXITIES OF THE DEMOCRATIC MANDATE." MIGRATION OBSERVATORY POLICY PRIMER, COMPAS, UNIVERSITY OF OXFORD, MARCH 2011.

DUNCAN GARDHAM (17 JANUARY 2012). "ABU QATADA CANNOT BE DEPORTED TO JORDAN, EUROPEAN JUDGES RULE". THE DAILY TELEGRAPH. RETRIEVED 23 FEBRUARY 2012.

ELECTORAL ADMINISTRATION ACT 2006, SECTION 18

FORD, ROBERT. "ACCEPTABLE AND UNACCEPTABLE IMMIGRANTS: THE ETHNIC HIERARCHY IN BRITISH IMMIGRATION PREFERENCES." JOURNAL OF ETHNIC AND MIGRATION STUDIES 37 (2011): 1017-1037.

GORDON, IAN, KATHLEEN SCANLON, TONI TRAVERS, AND CHRISTINE WHITEHEAD. "ECONOMIC IMPACT ON THE LONDON AND UK ECONOMY OF AN EARNED REGULARISATION OF IRREGULAR MIGRANTS TO THE UK." LONDON SCHOOL OF ECONOMICS, LONDON, 2009.

HAINMUELLER, JENS AND MICHAEL J. HISCOX. "ATTITUDES TOWARD HIGHLY SKILLED AND LOW-SKILLED IMMIGRATION: EVIDENCE FROM A SURVEY EXPERIMENT." AMERICAN POLITICAL SCIENCE REVIEW 104 (2010), 61-84.

HANSEN, JOHN MARK. "INDIVIDUALS, INSTITUTIONS, AND PUBLIC PREFERENCES OVER PUBLIC FINANCE." AMERICAN POLITICAL SCIENCE REVIEW 92 (1998): 513-531

IMMIGRATION RULES PARAGRAPHS 276ADE-276DH

IPSOS MORI. "UK BORDER AGENCY PUBLIC ATTITUDES SURVEY." IPSOS MORI, LONDON, 2009.

IPSOS MORI. "IMMIGRATION AND ASYLUM." POLL PREPARED ON BEHALF OF THE MIGRATION OBSERVATORY. IPSOS MORI, LONDON, 2011.
LIST OF THE TREATIES COMING FROM THE SUBJECT-MATTER: HUMAN RIGHTS (CONVENTION AND PROTOCOLS ONLY). RETRIEVED 21 FEBRUARY 2009.

MCLAREN, LAUREN. "CAUSE FOR CONCERN? THE IMPACT OF IMMIGRATION ON POLITICAL TRUST." POLICY NETWORK, LONDON, 2010.
NATIONAL CENTRE FOR SOCIAL RESEARCH. "BRITISH SOCIAL ATTITUDES SURVEY 2003." NATIONAL CENTRE FOR SOCIAL RESEARCH, LONDON, 2003.

NATIONALITY, IMMIGRATION AND ASYLUM ACT 2002

OVEY, CLARE; ROBIN C.A. WHITE. THE EUROPEAN CONVENTION ON HUMAN RIGHTS. OXFORD UNIVERSITY PRESS. PP. 1-3. ISBN 978-01- 992881-0-6.

RIENZO, CINZIA AND CARLOS VARGAS-SILVA. "MIGRANTS IN THE UK: AN OVERVIEW." MIGRATION OBSERVATORY BRIEFING, COMPAS, UNIVERSITY OF OXFORD, SEP 2011.

SIDES, J. AND J. CITRIN. "EUROPEAN OPINION ABOUT IMMIGRATION." BRITISH JOURNAL OF POLITICAL SCIENCE 37, NO. 3 (2007): 477-504.

THE EUROPEAN CONVENTION ON HUMAN RIGHTS (ECHR)

THE HUMAN RIGHTS ACT 1998

THE UNIVERSAL DECLARATION OF HUMAN RIGHTS

TRANSATLANTIC TRENDS. "TRANSATLANTIC TRENDS: IMMIGRATION, TOPLINE DATA 2010." GERMAN MARSHALL FUND, WASHINGTON DC, 2011.

YOUGOV/THE SUN. SURVEY ON IMMIGRATION ATTITUDES PREPARED ON BEHALF OF THE SUN. YOUGOV, LONDON, 2010.

HTTP://WWW.AMNESTY.ORG.UK/

HTTP://WWW.BBC.CO.UK/NEWS/UK-POLITICS-18384543

HTTP://WWW.DAILYMAIL.CO.UK/NEWS/ARTICLE-2279842/THERESA-MAY-HOME-SECRETARY-VOWS-CRUSH-JUDGES-REVOLT-RUSHING-TOUGH-NEW-LAWS.HTML

HTTP://WWW.DAILYMAIL.CO.UK/NEWS/ARTICLE-2015898/SQUATTERS-RIGHTS-LAW-GRANTS-ILLEGAL-IMMIGRANTS-RIGHT-STAY-14-YEARS-SCRAPPED.HTML

HTTP://WWW.EQUALITYHUMANRIGHTS.COM/

HTTP://WWW.GUARDIAN.CO.UK/COMMENTISFREE/LIBERTYCENTRAL/2009/JAN/13/IMMIGRATION-ASYLUM-ACT

HTTP://WWW.GUARDIAN.CO.UK/COMMENTISFREE/LIBERTYCENTRAL/2009/JAN/14/HUMAN-RIGHTS-ACT

HTTP://WWW.GUARDIAN.CO.UK/COMMENTISFREE/LIBERTYCENTRAL/2009/JAN/15/NATIONALITY-IMMIGRATION-ASYLUM-ACT

HTTP://WWW.GUARDIAN.CO.UK/SOCIETY/2002/OCT/24/ASYLUM.POLITICS

HTTP://WWW.LEGISLATION.GOV.UK/

HTTP://WWW.TELEGRAPH.CO.UK/NEWS/UKNEWS/LAW-AND-ORDER/8643483/IMMIGRATION-LOOPHOLE-SET-TO-BE-CLOSED.HTML

HTTP://EN.WIKIPEDIA.ORG/WIKI/ARTICLE_8_OF_THE_EUROPEAN_CONVENTION_ON_HUMAN_RIGHTS

HTTPS://EN.WIKIPEDIA.ORG/WIKI/EUROPEAN_CONVENTION_ON_HUMAN_RIGHTS

HTTP://IMMIGRATIONMATTERS.CO.UK/14-YEAR-LONG-STAY-CONCESSION-TO-BE-CLOSED.HTML

HTTP://MIGRATIONOBSERVATORY.OX.AC.UK/REPORTS/THINKING-BEHIND-NUMBERS-UNDERSTANDING-PUBLIC-OPINION-IMMIGRATION-BRITAIN

HTTP://WWW.PUBLICATIONS. PARLIAMENT.UK/PA/LD200809/LDHANSRD/TEXT/90115W0003.HTML

HTTP://UKHUMANRIGHTSBLOG.COM/2012/06/13/ARTICLE-8-AND-A-HALF-WIDER-THAN-THOUGHT-BUT-WILL-IT-WORK/

HTTP://WWW.UKBA.HOMEOFFICE.GOV.UK/183

꿈꾸는 불법자들

2024년 8월 31일
저자 최고야
편집 김광철
번역 김보람
교열 강경은
북디자인 최고야

프로파간다
전북 군산시 구영4길 16-2 (영화동)
www.graphicmag.co.kr

ISBN 978-89-98143-86-2

Illegal Dreamers

August 2024
Author Choi, Goya
Editing Kim, Kwangchul
Translation Kim, Boram
Proof Reading Kang, Kyungeun
Book Design Choi, Goya

propaganda
16-2 Guyeong 4-gil, Gunsan-si, Jeollabuk-do, South Korea
www.graphicmag.co.kr

ISBN 978-89-98143-86-2

Printed in Korea

reddot award 2016
winner

이 인쇄물은 2016년 레드닷 어워드에서 수상한 프로젝트의 한글 번역본으로 재출판되었습니다.

This publication is a reissued Korean translation of a project that won the Reddot Award in 2016.

값 20,000원
02320
9 788998 143862
ISBN 978-89-98143-86-2